AUDACITY TO Shine

LESSONS from WOMEN of COLOR
LIFE, FAITH and BUSINESS

I dedicate this book to the unsung heroes and mentors in my life who were light bearers for me.
They brightened my paths to healing, change, and transformation.

— C Nicole Henderson

Acknowledgements

C Nicole Henderson:

I give honor to my grandmother and family for providing me with the life lessons that made me the woman who I am today. To my son, Nic, who is always the forever love in my heart, you have challenged me to shine, and more, abundantly. Honor and glory to God, my Abba, my Father, for this project and for His prophetic words, visions, and dreams that I am entrusted with by the Holy Spirit. To the amazing nine authors who are a part of this anthology, thank you; you are the best light bearers in the world. To Kasper Harris, Gifft Grafix, for the amazing book cover. I am most grateful for my countless readers and proofers. Last but definitely not least, to BFF Publishing House and its wonderful editing staff.

Marlene Carson:

When I think about my journey and those who have touched my life, those who lifted me when I was down and helped to balance my life so that I didn't get puffed up, there are far too many people to name. However, the ones who mean the most to me gave me the strength, tenacity, and resiliency to be who I am today. To my children who mean the world to me, you are the reason why I have the audacity to shine.

Sai Lena Willis:

I thank God for allowing me to be a part of His plan and purpose on Earth. To C.D. Roberts, for being in alignment with me and putting me in the position to SHINE, I am forever grateful, and I thank you. To my son,

Dominic, for believing in me and always supporting me. You show me the best of myself and I am honored to be your mother. To the little girl who I used to be, I dedicate this to you, because without your strength to survive and willingness to live, I would not have the audacity to shine bright. To my grandmother, Marva, you are the greatest of all time.

Jacqueline "LuLu" Brown:

I dedicate my chapter to my shero: my mom. She is the force in my life that encouraged me to "be Lulu" and be audacious enough to shine. To my Husband, Sisters, children, family, and close friends; thank you from the bottom of my heart.

Toyin Fadina:

I would like to thank God, the Almighty, who has granted me the opportunity to become a writer, for His courage and strength to speak and live in my truth.

I dedicate my chapter to every strong woman who is living in silence due to a mental health condition. My chapter was written to raise awareness of the mental health effects of a global pandemic to help reduce the stigma around mental health conditions and increase support for those who have them.

I give honor to my grandmother, Mrs. Rosie Mae Oliver. Her legacy of never giving up, no matter what gave me the fuel to keep on keeping on during the pandemic. I thank my lovely daughter, who has always been instrumental and by my side on my S.M.A.R.T. journey. Special thanks to my strong and faithful mother, Annette Fadina. It would be impossible to list all names, but my gratitude goes out to all who supported me through this process.

April Sanders:

Jesus, I would not be caught dead without You. This chapter is dedicated to my mommy and those who suffer from mental illness. After the loss of my grandmother, I never imagined that anyone else could ever hold the same wisdom. Deborah Lee (Mama D), you are my angel here on Earth. To my amazing children, I am grateful that the fruit of my womb has been blessed with your life. To the fuel that keeps my fire LIT—Change Church.

Conswella Smith:

Minister Quanda Jackson, Pastor Michael and First Lady Arlene Thomas, Coach and Counselor Natolie Warren, C Nicole Henderson

Wanda Pearson:

Dennis Pearson, Danielle Thompson, Tori Logan, Judi Smith-Ogletree, Sharryn Harewood, Evie Liverman Fleming, Angela Sims

Foreword

I am the fifth of eight children. I worked in corporate America for over twenty-five years. I've owned my business for eight years and it has not always been easy to let my light shine. There were times when I was afraid of, intimidated by, or threatened by the thought of outshining others or shining my own light. Once I broke free, I refused to dim my light anymore. That was when I met C Nicole. I saw her light the first time we met at an event and we've shone our lights both individually and collectively ever since.

Everyone has a light that shines bright within. However, when we perceive the world through our five senses to search for peace, fulfillment, and happiness, we often forget about the light that has been inside of us all along.

In order for your light to shine bright, you must first learn to see it with full clarity.

Letting my light shine has not always come naturally to me. My doubts and fears caused me to ask myself, How dare you shine? Because of bad past experiences, any time I shone my light, I was reminded of darker times.

Something I've been playing with and discovering over the last few years is just how bright I can let my inner light shine. This little light of mine, I'm gonna let it shine...

We all have that inner light; that inner spark; that space in which some say divine light fills us; that space where consciousness resides; that thing that gives us life and, I'd say, purpose. We have this inner light, and part of our journey is recognizing it. We must recognize it; coax it out of hiding; take ownership of it; take responsibility for it; play with it; and discover how it has blessed us with our own unique gifts to the world. Then, we must figure out how to use these gifts in a way that is deeply fulfilling. It is the light that, when cultivated and allowed to be expressed, brings sustained joy.

But here's something I've noticed. Maybe you've noticed it, too. As I start to step into my light, as I nurture and nourish and then shine the crap out of my light and feel SO GOOD in my body, other people notice.

Our inner light—that piece of us that activates consciousness within our bodies and that scientists still don't understand—is unlimited. It is Source. It is in each and every one of us and it connects us. This same light within me is also within you, and because of the light we share, we are one. When I shine my light brighter and grow bigger, you do not have to become smaller. You can be big, and I can be big, or we can be small—or medium. This source is unlimited. C Nicole knows this source and has had the AUDACITY TO SHINE, regardless of her past and what life has thrown her way. In the years that I've known her, I've seen her glow, her shine, and her light, which is why she is the perfect person to share these amazing authors who also have the AUDACITY TO SHINE.

I'm honored to write this foreword and to know C Nicole. So, what do you do when you notice that your inner light is being dimmed? As a highly sensitive person, I can feel when my inner light is being asked or forced to be smaller because someone else fears that my light might outshine theirs. This book will help you to have the AUDACITY TO SHINE your light, and one of these stories may inspire you to keep shining through the good, the bad, and the ugly.

I hope that you enjoy your time with C Nicole Henderson and all of the coauthors. Their true stories and miracles have produced life-changing outcomes for them, and I pray that they change your life, too.

Becky A. Davis
Chief Bosspreneur®
Author of 40 Days of Prayer for My Business: Think Big, Pray Hard and Wait Expectantly

Contents

Preface

This book is for you if you have gone through any struggles in your life and are ready to be inspired, motivated, and empowered to live triumphantly after allowing tragedy, past hurts, victim mentality, or even life failures hold you back. It is not a coincidence that you are reading this book at this moment. This is your season for change. You, too, have a purposeful light waiting to shine.

Matthew 5:14-16 reads, "You are the light of the world—like a city on a hilltop that cannot be hidden. No one lights a lamp and then puts it under a basket. Instead, a lamp is placed on a stand, where it gives light to everyone in the house. In the same way, let your good deeds (light) shine out for all to see, so that everyone will praise your heavenly Father."

So many of us have had our light hidden, dimmed, or completely extinguished by the pain and hurdles of life. May we take our mournings, pains, hang-ups, addictions, poor mindsets, and life struggles, and turn them around with a renewed mind, hope, humility, overcoming spirit, and victories; and use them for His glory to be a beacon of light, hope, love, joy, and transformation for others. The dedicated authors in this project have done just that. They have turned their life struggles, shortcomings, hurdles, pains, and unbearable circumstances around for themselves and for the others whose lives they have changed in so many ways.

I was abandoned, rejected, denied, abused, left with nothing, and unemployed several times. I raised my son as a divorced parent for twenty years, lost loved ones, and experienced health challenges and heartbreak, but God. I am still here to let my light shine so that others will see His glory upon my face and grateful life, and know that I am blessed not by my own might, but because I am His beloved daughter. I will share more of my transformation story of walking in faithFULLNESS and building successful businesses in the midst of loss and lack. My chapter is "The Audacity to Living Your Dreams: A Walk of Faithfulness in Relationships, Life, and Marketplace."

My life changed when these nine ladies said YES! We laughed and cried together as we created this collaboration. The authors will walk you through their struggles to life success by sharing their stories with you. You may see yourself in their stories or even a glimpse of your current situation. These women are beacons of light. Know that you are not alone. You are not forgotten, lost, unloved, or worthless. No matter what happened in your past, I surely declare and decree a new present and future and a new you in the name of Jesus. Yes, you have the Audacity to Shine!

We challenge you to not only read this book, but to participate in the Audacity to Shine Round Table Discussions to go to the next level of healing, growth, development, and freedom.

Each author has a life changing message that was developed from their chapter to expand the discussion of their story into a life lesson and real life experience of reset and transformation.

We encourage you to also read the book with groups, give copies to friends and family, and share the beautiful life-changing and powerful messages within these pages.

Nicole Henderson

"Alleviate your obstacles in man and elevate your success by faith."
— Conswella Smith

Chapter 1
C Nicole Henderson

The Audacity of Living Your Dreams

"A Walk of Faithfulness in Relationships, Life, and Marketplace."

Walking in faithfulness and building businesses in the midst of loss and growing pains is not an easy task. However, I felt that my upbringing and faith prepared me to endure life's hurdles and to overcome them. I am a faith walker in everything that I do. You'd better have faith when you charter into unknown territories and waters. I am reminded of the nursery rhyme, "Row, Row, Row Your Boat"... the sentiment that life is but a dream. The boat represents our lives. Our lives can be enhanced by our dreams. This is one way that God speaks to us—in our dreams and visions. He does so in order to give us directions to follow our paths (purpose) and streams (sources) toward greater, fulfilled lives. God is our supreme captain and we are the co-captains of our lives. I want you to know that you can have it all. We can bridge the gap between faith and marketplace. My life lessons began far sooner than a young child should have to deal with adult issues.

When I was a ten-year-old girl, I remember sitting on the floor in my grandmother's bedroom while leaning against her bed with my tape recorder in hand. I recorded myself singing Billie Holiday's "God Bless the Child" over and over again. I also hoped to teach myself how to carry a note and sing. Music was a big influence in my life. I grew up with block parties and jazz concerts in the city streets of Harlem. The jazz players led to my interest in playing an instrument. I played the clarinet from the fifth grade until my senior year of high school. I have fond memories of days in the marching and jazz bands.

My mother and father were not in my life after I moved in with my grandmother. I learned how to take care of myself, and I wanted more from life. I wanted my own money and choices. This caused me to learn early about striving to get what you want and working very hard for it. My grandmother loved me dearly. Growing up in my adolescent years, I did not have parents to guide me along my journey. I had to navigate as best as I could. There were times when I was rowing very hard against the tides; however, at some point, I learned to glide and realized that there is grace over the grind to get ahead in life. When we are kingdom believers, we lean not into our own understanding. We seek the face of God in prayer to guide our lives through life milestones to more productive journeys and steady streams of income.

Hiding in the Shadows of My Own Light

To be honest with you, I did not realize the fullness of my own light until I began to write this story. I was hiding so much without even knowing it. The first cover for this book displayed a woman standing in the corner of a room; the woman had her back turned and was looking at sunlight. For too many years, I have been silent and sitting in the shadows of my own life. Many may feel that I was bold and out in the open, but I really felt like I played a leading role in my own story, going back and forth into the safety of the dressing room that was my life. I first found solace and comfort in a closet as a little girl. I would read books while sitting on the floor of the closet to escape from the life that I lived with my mother in Harlem. She was a heroin user and would go into the bathroom to shoot up. I would sit on the cold floor and lean against the bathroom door, crying and begging her not to do so. My efforts felt fruitless, so I escaped into other worlds and places by reading.

My stepfather was a drug dealer, but he was very kind to me. I was raised to not share certain things about my family's business, such as the fights, arguments, drugs, and parties. It was not until I was an adult that I even shared that my family had been held at gunpoint and robbed in our apartment. I felt that my survival and theirs was in my hands at that moment. As I watched from the chair I sat in, I could not show fear to the two guys who were robbing my stepdad. Even though I was only six years old, I felt like I needed to shock them by doing something different. I screamed at those robbers, "Get the hell out of my house and leave us alone!" They left after getting the money from my stepdad's pants pocket. Who knew that New York City would prepare me for my greatest moments of survival: leaving the big city to live in a country coastal town, then moving to the big city of Atlanta and losing my daddy forever. My grandmother raised me from the age of seven. I would soon experience abandonment and rejection, which instilled even greater fear and anxiety in me. Fear was present in my life in a major way, showing up on more than one occasion, and affected me well into my adulthood.

In recent years, I sought psychotherapy and counseling to overcome my seemingly chronic fear and the things that were holding me back from shining and truly being my best self. I did not have many examples of true self-love in my life. Faith overcomes fear, yet I had allowed my faith to become bigger than my fears. While visiting my grandmother one summer, my mother called. I was in the hallway listening to the phone call and heard my mother tell my grandmother not to send me back to New York. I was so heartbroken and angry. I was angry because this caused me to instantly lose the relationship I had with my father. My mother never told me, nor him, where I was. I loved my dad very much and we had a good relationship while I lived in Harlem. When I would visit him in the Bronx, he would cherish me with love, gifts, and shopping trips. I was a daddy's girl for sure.

I searched for my father and found him thirty years later, but he had passed away. I remember that day perfectly. I had listened to an archived sermon from Dr. Cooper of Mount Paran Church of God that had been recorded exactly one year before. Cooper proclaimed in his sermon, "The thing that you have been asking God for is already done. Do not ask Him anymore. It is settled." God heard my plea and He answered me that day. A longtime male friend called me shortly thereafter out of the blue (there are no coincidences with God!) and asked about my father. I was quite perturbed by him asking me and I caught an attitude with him. I went online right after ending the phone call and searched for my dad, Milton Carroll. His name, address, and birthday, as well as information about his life and wife, were all displayed right in front of my eyes thirty years after I overheard the call between my mother and grandmother. Sometimes, we have to wait thirty years, but surely, God will eventually provide us with an answer. I was so happy and overjoyed that God had answered my long-awaited prayer. I know that I am not the only child who has lost one parent by the hand or decision of the other. I have come to terms with my mother's decision to leave me at my grandmother's house. I later learned, through God's revelation, that my mother was only able to carry me so far in this world. She did not have the capacity to do much more. She achieved her purpose, which was carrying me into this world. God knows her struggles and pain. He gives all of us the power of forgiveness, which I so liberally extended to my mother and father over time.

Still, God had answered my prayer to find my father. We have to be careful to be specific in our prayers. God is faithful and knows what we need better than we do. I hope to one day write a film about my upbringing with my dad in Harlem, the Bronx, and Manhattan. What made the experience of rediscovering my dad even more hurtful was finding out that he had lived in the same building on Grand Avenue for all those years we had been apart, just in a different apartment. It was a godly miracle that I found him thirty years later, just months before I had planned to take a trip back to New York City. I will be sure to include the amazing story in the movie script.

Great is Thy Faithfulness

My grandmother never received any financial, emotional, or physical support from my parents. I adored my grandmother; she took great care of me and showered me with love. She taught me my first lesson on faithfulness. She was very faithful to me, to our family, to God, and to her church. I was required to get on the Sunday school bus every week to attend Bethel Baptist Church. I came to know God at a very young age and had a sincere relationship with the Father and Son. I served on the usher board and in the youth choir. My hometown Baptist church did not teach much about the Holy Spirit. I would cry in church when I felt moved. I felt something in my heart, even though I had not been taught much about this feeling. I was an avid dreamer and had visions from a very young age. I dreamed of being able to take care of myself one day and not having to depend on anyone for help, especially financially. My grandmother would say that I was "too independent."

I learned my second lesson on faithfulness through my experience with education. I knew that I would need a career, and education was my ticket to success. I was very smart, I made great grades, and I excelled, especially in math and science. I was a gifted orator. I did not realize until later in life that I had a gift for speaking and writing; these things came to me easily and I was good at them. I spoke all over town for various events and at 4-H competitions. The 4-H leaders and teachers were mentors and positive influences in my life, so I enjoyed hanging around them. I would learn speeches that were seven to ten pages long and give them during various church services and events. I loved to watch dramas, dance, act, speak, run, and bake with my grandmother. She was my rock and best friend.

My third lesson of faithfulness related to finances; I learned about finances in my early years by watching my grandmother make ends meet. We never missed meals and I don't remember any utilities ever being cut off. I learned about delayed gratification and living within my means. She would purchase things with credit, but she always made sure to pay her obligations. She kept a keepsake stash in a handkerchief in her bosom. That was her secret bank, but she would put money into her savings as well. I wished that she and my uncles would have taught me more about finances. If so, I would not have made some of the mistakes that I did in my adult life. I would have understood retirement and the value of savings. I learned from a successful business coach, Daniel Ally, that how much money we make matters, but what matters even more is how much we keep. Cash flow is real and imperative to successful business growth.

The Struggle of Ministry Over Marketplace

My twenties and thirties came with both challenges and wins. By the time I turned twenty-five, I was married to my college sweetheart. I was in graduate school, working to obtain a master's degree in Public Administration. I loved my college years. I spent most of them in apartments because during my very first semester, my dorm building was burned down by another student who was freebasing drugs on the second floor. I learned the value of working hard to pursue my dreams and goals and studying hard to make ends meet. I was grooming myself to become a city or county manager. I later realized that city and county managers did not have much job security and that they moved around a lot. So, I pursued community development planning and some grant work and later became the director of the county government department. I had the big title with loads of responsibility, no time to take off from work to enjoy my son, and a very low salary. I was twenty-nine years old with great power and abilities, but I was making under forty thousand dollars per year. I wanted and needed more. Raising a son as a divorced mother was not easy. However, I had my family to lean on and my son would visit his father twice a month, which hugely helped me. I felt that there was more to life than what I had going on at the time. My personal relationship with God had grown by leaps and bounds. I had joined a spirit-led church that taught straight from the Bible. I was active in ministry and leadership. This was the first time that I helped a church become a 501c3 nonprofit organization. I was learning so much in this area. After losing my grandmother in January of 2002, I moved back to Atlanta, but I knew that I was done working as an employee in the government sector. I felt like a little girl who was lost in a big city. I was interested in teaching and did so for a few years with a focus on the early childhood age group. I worked various odd jobs and took on some contract work. It was during this season that I was hit with layoffs and work that was not fulfilling.

As my faith grew, so did my confidence. I now believed that I could step out on my own and start my own business. I had become an independent consultant for Mary Kay Cosmetics, but I didn't really understand the team building components and the mindset needed to run a successful business. I knew how to sell, but it takes more than a good sales pitch to achieve real growth and team development. I struggled to balance working for another company and building my own business. I tried several other direct selling companies over the years with both great and not-so-great results. It takes more than discipline to run a successful business. Running a successful business requires skill and knowledge in sales, bookkeeping, sales funnels, strategic marketing plans, team development, and much more.

This was the start of my greatest struggle with the dichotomy between my ministry work and my business work. I would start and stop many companies, using the excuse that the church ministry needed me and I did not have time to engage in both. I felt like I had to choose one over the other.

I was not the only person struggling with this dichotomy between ministry work and career or business work. Even in the Bible, many of the disciples had trades that they pursued and became successful in. I am not saying that there are no places or opportunities for ministry-only work— churches and missions serve this purpose. This work is essential for those who are called to do so. I am referring to the many laypersons who are struggling to simultaneously serve God and pursue their dreams in the marketplace. I know that I am called to this group of faith walkers in business.

Your passion, purpose, and mission are all tied to serving and operating as a disciple and servant leader. In 1967, Dr. Martin Luther King Jr. gave a speech called "What is Your Life's Blueprint?" He stated, "Be a bush if you can't be a tree. If you can't be a highway, just be a trail. If you can't be a sun, be a star. For it isn't by size that you win or fail. Be the best of whatever you are." So, no matter what you do, be the best at it and be the best witness to souls while you are there. If you are a stockbroker, investment banker, doctor, teacher, accountant, or glass blower, you can serve and grow right where you are planted in your work mission and profession. My previous internal medicine physician would display scriptures on the board in his office and pray with his clients. This was a true example of a Christian business owner who was intentional about his faith. You are not compromising the gospel by serving in your business or profession.

According to the Theology of Business Institute, "If God has called you into business, please don't wish you were called somewhere else. The marketplace is a great place for Christians right now." Many of us will become the only messenger who others are exposed to in the workplace. Here, one can witness Christ with less influence or pressure from one particular denomination. The environment can be more open for people to engage in conversation about what they may be struggling with and exchange sound wisdom and encouragement without being "churchy" or heavily emphasizing religion.

I am clear in my role as a marketplace minister and servant leader. I minister to my clients when they request prayer or encouragement. I started teaching online courses on visions and dreams in 2011. I offer coaching sessions. I am certified as a Christian teacher and ordained as a prophet. I created the Grace to Completion platform for those who have gifts inside of them to assist them in uncovering those gifts and equip them to carry out the missions, purposes, and plans that God has for them. My platform is a safe place in which faith walkers can experience, hear, and know the voice of God to direct their pathways, visions, and dreams.

2011, as a whole, was a true turning point in my life. I left my job to start a consulting company that summer, only to go back to my former job three months later because I was afraid. I did not want to spend another Christmas with my son possibly lacking anything, or with us having just enough to get by on our bills. After returning to work, I was released from that job in January of 2012 and the company soon went out of business. I was not surprised by their closure. I had a dream about the company in which I saw an empty cash register. This was not the first layoff I had experienced since living in Atlanta, but it truly was my last, because I had ventured toward the American dream of business ownership—for real this time. It took me a minute to find my niche and create profitable systems. I did not embark on this journey alone. I joined communities of female business owners and sought coaching and developmental assistance along the way. Most importantly, I elevated my mindset. I gained a fuller business understanding and raised my spiritual maturity above simple religious acts and mindsets.

I remember getting the call from HR while driving home. We all know what an HR call at the end of the day usually means to an employee. I was smiling from ear to ear as I listened to the voice at the other end of the line. I had just stated earlier that day to my graphic artist that I wanted to find time to create my vision, develop my dream courses, and scale my nonprofit consulting business to a greater level. I knew this time that my layoff was not in vain. It was worth it. I was humming to the beat of Beyoncé's "Love on Top." God is the one I need, He is the one I love, He is always there. He puts MY love on top!

"Love on Top" became my anthem. It gave me the motivation to develop love for myself first and provided me with the energy to keep going. I have always loved that song. Beyoncé is a phenomenal artist and a shrewd businesswoman. I credit her for her long-term success and how she has overcome her struggles on a very public platform. According to Wikipedia , she changes her outfits four times in the "Love on Top" music video. This represents the four changes in key and the high vocal ranges during the song's chorus. We have four seasons in a year, all of which can have highs and lows. I have experienced both over the last nine years.

I know what it is like both to have and to not have for myself and my household. I am a tither and a giver. This statement is not an argument on whether others should tithe or not, but it truly has been my personal course of trusting God for greater and more in my life. All things belong to God. We are only the stewards of our worldly possessions. When you are living out your dreams, visions, and purpose, increase is just the added benefit. You are grateful and humble to be a blessing to others as well as to give and receive abundantly. I remember a time when I was laid off during my son's early childhood. We had no food in the fridge that day. I went into the home office, called out to God, and was reminded of His word in Psalms 37:25 which states that we shall not be forsaken nor begging for bread. Within fifteen minutes, I received a call from a friend who said that God told her to get groceries for me. She asked me to come over and pick them up from her house. She did not get me a few bags of groceries— she had gotten enough food to fiil my pantries and my fridge. God had already sent her before I had even asked. I am not sure how she knew I was not working at the time. God knows our every need. I know how it feels to lose hope or when your hope is deferred. The Holy Spirit is our comforter and Jesus is our hope when there is none. God is the way-maker.

As a faith walker, I seek the fullness of God in all that I do and all that He provides on my life path.

Due to the lessons that I have learned in this season of my journey, I have learned to smile in spite of the pain. I have learned that life is not easy, but living is worth it. I have learned how to say no and mean it. I learned the true meaning of the sentiments, "grace over grind" and "rest over strife." I learned that there is healing in tears. I learned that I own nothing—not my possessions, my assets, or my son. Everything belongs to God and we cannot out give God. He is the greatest giver. I have learned to take risks, with Christ as my CEO and I as his strategic partner and chief operations officer. I have learned to trust myself. I now have confidence and humility in my abilities, talents, and gifting, for they are for God's glory to use as He sees fit. I am grateful for so many things: the years of success that God has given to me, the health of my adult son, my loving relationship with my son, my growing six-figure businesses, and my financial stewardship.

Not long after I started teaching about visions and dreams, the Lord God called me the "Dream Revelator." I understand this title far greater today than I did some years ago. I taught students and ministry leaders online before doing so was popular in the US and internationally. I am called and ordained to inspire, influence, instruct, and impact the body of Christ and nonbelievers alike with messages of hope, joy, transformation, love, peace, reconciliation, salvation, and the good news. I am equipped to help others with the tools to grow deeper in their relationships with Christ; to understand the mysteries in the word of God that are hidden for them and not from them; to seek the keys to faith in relationships, careers or businesses, and stewardships. With the Grace to Completion platform and Envision Institute, we will build up Impactpreneurs in the marketplace and leaders and disciples in the Fivefold Ministry.

As I approach the next chapter of my life, I am grateful for and appreciative of you taking the time to read and benefit from these life stories of women who went from struggling to experiencing success. This is just the beginning of your journey—consider enrolling in the coaching platform and participating in our online community. We want to hear from you all and help you to walk in the faithFULLNESS of your life. Invite us for a chapter reading and course study with your book clubs, social groups, ministry groups, and work teams.

1 Corinthians 13:13: "But now faith, hope, and love remain—these three. The greatest of these is love."

"Failure will never overtake me if my determination to success is strong enough."
— Og Mandino

"Live in the present, for it is a gift....God takes care of our tomorrows."
— C Nicole Henderson

Chapter 2
Dr. Marlene Carson

This Little Light of Mine

Ever since I was a little girl, I've always had the spotlight. Being the youngest of five children automatically comes with a little extra attention. My brothers and sister used to say that I was "spoiled." Although I would never admit it to them, between you and me, baby, I was spoiled rotten. You see, my grandmother (my mother's mother) lived down the street from us. I would walk to her house, and when I got there, baby, she would give me anything I wanted. Much later in life, I realized that what I thought was provision was really protection—the protection of my potential. I believe that my grandmother knew some of the danger I faced as a girl. She kept me with her as much as possible. She spoke into my life and convinced me that I could do anything I set my mind to. Do you know your grandmother? Has she been instrumental in your life?

So, Grandma invested in my future. She tried her best to cultivate the gifts within me, chastise me without destroying me, and build me up when I felt like the world was tearing me down. However, the downside of being the youngest of five is that while all eyes were on me, no one really saw me. They watched me for the sake of protecting me, but had no true knowledge of who I was, who God created me to be. Because of their skewed perceptions, they didn't recognize certain signs that indicated when things were off within me.

Rejection, insecurity, and abandonment were my constant companions. My first experience with rejection happened when I was just eight years old. I wanted to go to the mall with my older sister, who we called "Sister." At that time, public transportation was twenty-five cents each way, so my sister told me to go ask Dad for the money. As usual, Mom was in the kitchen cooking and Dad was in their bedroom with the door shut. I knocked on the door.

"Daddy, may I please have fifty cents to go to the mall?" I asked him loudly.

"No, I don't have any money," he hollered back.

I walked away from the door, sobbing with my thumb in my mouth.

"What's wrong?" my sister asked. She had heard me crying.

"I can't go. Daddy said he doesn't have any money," I answered. She took me by the hand and sat me on the couch.

"Wait right here," she said. She knocked on Dad's door and called out to him. "Daddy, do you have a dollar? I want to go to the mall."

"Come on in," I heard my father tell her. He gave her the dollar without hesitation and we went to the mall. She was all smiles, but she didn't notice how devastated I was. Why did he give the dollar to her and not me?

I couldn't wait to be the only girl at home after my sister went off to college. I thought that things would be different for me and my dad when that happened. Boy, was I wrong, and I never understood how it would change my reality. At that point, I was left in a household filled with alcoholism and domestic violence. There were more questions than answers for a young girl with nowhere to turn. It wasn't until my father's death that I would finally get the answers I so desperately needed.

Let me ask you this: Can you pinpoint a time in your life when you felt rejected, insecure, or abandoned? How has that affected your life as an adult, an entrepreneur, a husband, or a wife? For me, rejection played an integral part in my life. The joy and innocence that I could once light up a room with had been dimmed by insecurity and rejection. The enemy of my soul had a plan to put my light out forever and he was using those closest to me to get the job done.

So, for years, I lived as a product of my environment. I still remember my parents partying, waking up us kids, and giving us quarters to dance for them. When I look back now, I find it interesting that I was the only one who received dollars to dance. I was always told how pretty and sexy I was, even as a child. Suddenly, I felt pretty and appreciated, and all of the emptiness disappeared for a brief time—until the predators made their moves. Those compliments led to the defilement of my body. Although I was never penetrated as a child, I can still see the hulking shadows of men as they overpowered me.

At the time, I didn't understand why I was told not to tell Momma that I had gotten twenty dollars just for sitting on my uncle's lap. It was a trusted family member who introduced me to the base act of a lap dance. Who would have ever thought that being the paid entertainment at our family functions as an eight-year-old would lead to me becoming a paid stripper at eighteen? Now, I realize that I was passed around at an early age by cousins, uncles, and family friends; they scattered pieces of me everywhere, leaving me broken and ashamed. With a life devoid of love, I was set up to fall for the first man who would say the words "I love you." When I finally heard those words, I didn't realize that they were a cloaked dagger that would eventually cut me to the core. When that man's true intentions were exposed, it came at a high price for me. He sold me in a New York City hotel for five hundred dollars to a man who didn't even care to know my name. I was nothing more than a piece of meat that was there to satisfy his appetite. So often, the vulnerable are deceived by pretenses of protection, provision, and prosperity which lead to prostitution, prohibition, and poverty. In that one dark moment, my innocence, my light, and my hope were ripped from my soul. The little girl who was once full of life, laughter, and joy was now full of bitterness.

From the first day I was sold, I continued to be trafficked in brothels, casinos, Quarter Horse shows, and golf outings. You name it! Wherever there were men, money, and alcohol, there was also exploitation.

I was being raped multiple times a day, becoming very angry, callous, and full of darkness. I fought with thoughts of murder and suicide on a daily basis. It's really dangerous how you can sit across the table from someone and smile at them while they are eating their dinner, meanwhile they don't even know that you are trying to figure out how to get them out of your life at any cost. I was on a fast track to self-destruction.

Did you know that there is a second definition of suicide? We know that the first definition of suicide is the ending of one's own life. There's another way to kill yourself, though. You can let the enemy destroy you by believing his lies and destroying yourself while you're still breathing. It's the life of a zombie, the existence of the living dead.

Honestly, I didn't care what I had to do in order to make it stop. I just wanted it to stop. I wanted to go back home to my mom, to the love and family that I knew, and see if I could find my light. I would smile at the man I hated for ruining my life. Then, there were times when I thought I loved him. Let me tell you, Stockholm syndrome may not be in the DSM (Diagnostic and Statistical Manual of Mental Disorders), but it is real. If you don't know what Stockholm syndrome is, it is described as a victim sharing an emotional bond with their perpetrator. If I had to self-diagnose, I would say that PTSD (Post Traumatic Stress Disorder), Stockholm syndrome, attention deficit disorder, and impostor syndrome have all been results of trauma. Dissociative disorders would have been accurate diagnoses, as well. I was all messed up. My mind, will, and emotions lived in a world so dark that I could no longer see my way out.

...or so I thought! But GOD!!!

The light of God will shine anywhere, even in the darkest night. When that light appears, those who are still living in blindness won't understand at first. When you are the one who has been touched by that light, those around you will be confused. They will say that there's something different about you. Has anyone ever said that to you? Your light is irresistible. That gift of beauty and light was given to you by your heavenly Father. The enemy seeks to destroy that light by perverting it and turning it into a tool of darkness. This is the environment that I came out of, but this is not where I came from. The light of God's truth illuminates the pathway of liberation, dispelling all matter of darkness and removing the cataracts from our spiritual eyes so that we may clearly see. For me, the light of truth shone through Jeremiah 29:11: "For I know the thoughts that I think toward you, saith the LORD, thoughts of peace, and not of evil, to give you an expected end." That scripture would continually prove its truth in my life through my environment, situations, and even my relationships.

My story—including my past, present, and future—was known in the mind of God even before I was formed in the womb. Preestablished in the mind of God, the many transitions, private victories, and public deliverances were all a part of the process—the process that doesn't necessarily lead me to a happy ending like a fairy tale, but to an expected end. With that in mind, my past once filled with shadows of intimidation and insecurity has now become my testimony, because a shadow doesn't exist unless a light— the light of God's truth—shines upon its subject. This truth shines within the world of adult entertainment, in abusive relationships, and even in the Christian church to dispel the darkness that is the home of deception.

"And ye shall know the truth, and the truth shall make you free" (John 8:32). I have known the true intimacy found in the light of God's truth, setting me free from strip clubs, escort services, and pimps who hang in the darkest of motels, as well as those who stand behind the most ornate pulpits. For years, this scripture has rang so loudly in my ear: "Let your light so shine before men, that they may see your good works, and glorify your Father who is in heaven" (Matthew 5:16).

I realize that the Lord has "sent me to bind up the brokenhearted, to proclaim freedom for the captives and release from darkness for the prisoners because [He] has anointed me to proclaim good news to the poor" (Isaiah 61:1). But I was afraid, due to imposter syndrome, that I wasn't enough, not good enough, not smart enough. But the Lord kept speaking to me through His word, His people, and His provision. I began to embrace change, focus on myself, and build up my most holy faith. I have now carried the light of God all over the world, dispelling the darkness. I have sat with those in the crack house and those in the C-suite. During the COVID-19 pandemic, people were losing their jobs, and churches and organizations were closing by the thousands every day. This girl, once full of insecurity, rejection, and abandonment issues, received a call from the White House.

"You have been appointed by the President of The United States," the caller on the phone said to me. Yes! Now, my light shines in government, radiating once again to dispel the darkness. So, I take this little light of mine everywhere I go, and this, my friend, is why I have the Audacity to Shine!

"Know that you are chosen and stand in the power and authority that comes with being chosen."
— JLB, The Lulu Experience

Chapter 3
Stacy Bryant

FDLC – Fight Dirty Live Clean

Destiny is inevitable. How one chooses to arrive there is simply a matter of choice. How you go through the process determines the outcome.

Why is this happening to me?

It was the absolute worst day of my entire life. I really thought I had some bad times, but this day topped it all. Honestly, there have been some really bad days in my life, but this day took the cake.

My doctor looked me in the eyes and told me that I might not live to see my next birthday, that I could be dead within six months. I clearly remember my doctor's mouth moving and myself trying to understand what he was really saying.

Although I felt like my doctor had just waged a war on me, I walked out of his office the perfect representation of confidence. No one would have guessed how shattered I really was.

Let me take you back a little.

Spending a lot of time catering to your mental health and healing your emotional needs can really change your mindset.

I had finally gotten a promotion. I was running my own supply room, taking courses, and really excelling in my career. I was really loving the US Army at this time. My kids were doing amazing. They were enjoying life so much that I went to bed and woke up with a permanent smile on my face each and every day.

I had built a coaching business from the facilitation groups that I started, which focused on sexual assault and domestic violence. I had gotten trained and become certified as an Equal Employment Opportunity Representative and was able to contract with the military to provide my coaching services. Life was definitely good.

When you do the work to improve your mental health, you cannot expect to see immediate changes. Although immediate change can happen, true transformation will likely take time. You must be very consistent and persistent with the methods you choose in order for more positive messages to come into your subconscious mind. As soon as these transformations become apparent, you will feel motivated to keep moving forward. Keep at it, though, because these changes are lifelong, powerful, and well worth waiting for!

This is not to say that pressure, stress, and other things will not arise in your life. They will. However, continue to follow the new practices you have built around a healthy mindset and you will be able to approach any new challenges with vigor.

Why do I say that? Not too long after all of these amazing things began to transpire in my life, the biggest bombshell was dropped. I had just signed another reenlistment contract with the Army. With this new contract, I was able to take several months off from work to attend college. That meant no physical training, no formation, no work call, no green uniform. I could walk around like a civilian. I was in total heaven. That was an absolutely amazing and productive time in my life. My business skyrocketed to its peak at that time, as well. I had the time to commit to speaking engagements, which opened the door to more clients. It was a really good time for Coach Stacy Enterprises.

About halfway through my time off, I also decided to visit a real doctor. No offense to military doctors, but civilian life is totally different from the structured, organized life I had become accustomed to. While on active duty, you visit military doctors only. So, while on my sabbatical, I found a civilian doctor and made an appointment at my own expense. The appointment went great, but he scheduled a loop electrosurgical excision procedure due to my abnormal pap smear results and history. I had no idea that my staging process had begun.

After two days, a nurse called back and asked me to come in for my results. I could not, for the life of me, understand why I would need to go in, especially so soon, but I gladly scheduled an appointment and went in. When I arrived at the doctor's office, I immediately got a nagging feeling in the pit of my stomach, which I automatically ignored. Once I was called back into an examination room, I could not wait to get my test results so that I could move on to my next appointment.

When the doctor came in, he looked as if he had seen a ghost, but smiled at me. He asked how I was doing and began to explain the test he had performed. I still feel dizzy and nauseous when I think about that day. As the doctor started to speak, my mind trailed off. I could hear him, but I was not fully hearing him at the same time. Suddenly, I zoned back in.

"Did you say cancer?" I asked.

"Yes, ma'am, I did," he replied.

I immediately asked if we could stop for a second.

"Sir, I cannot have cancer. I will lose my job. Please tell me that is not what you just said," I pleaded.

"Sergeant Bryant, I understand. From what I am looking at, you may not live to see your next birthday, but we do need to get you scheduled for a PET scan as soon as possible. Are you available tomorrow?"

"Sir, I do not think you heard what I said. I cannot have cancer. Why do I need to come back?"

I would love to say that all the mental health skills I had learned kicked in at this moment, but no, they did not. I lost it at that point. When I finally came to, there was a nurse standing over me with a box of tissues in her hand.

She asked if I was okay and if the doctor could resume. At that point, I was numb. I told her that we could finish.

I sat in silence for the remainder of the appointment. To this day, I am really not sure of everything the doctor said—I was in another world. I only remember that I had to be back the next morning at 9 a.m.; I left and went straight home to bed. I canceled my remaining appointments for the rest of the day and lost myself in tears again. At that moment, I began to have flashbacks from six years ago. I then got nervous that I was going to relive my depression. So, I threw some water on my face and began to complete some homework assignments.

While suffering through this, the guy who I had been dating for the last six years came down on new orders. When he told me he was about to leave, I was sad. I thought we had been together for so long that we would always be together. Six years was the longest someone had ever remained in my life. As he prepared to leave, we talked about all of the ways that we would stay in touch once he left the country. My gut was doing a dance again—a serious dance. I prepared myself for his departure, but was hopeful that our relationship would withstand the distance.

The day finally arrived for him to leave. I saw him off at the airport and that was it. I went home and cried, but decided that everything would be okay. His flight would be very long, so I could not stay up and wait to hear that he made it. The next day, I went downstairs to prepare dinner. When I came back up, I saw that I had missed a call from him. I tried calling back, but the call went straight to voicemail. Wow, I cannot believe I missed his call, I thought. Then, I saw the dreadful text:

Why are you not answering?

Four days later, I got an email:

Hey Baby, I tried to call you,

I do not know if you got my message but I'm sorry I could not ever get over some things in our relationship. I do love you and your kid's, but I'm sorry we can't be together anymore and I'm not coming back. tell the kids I love and miss them, but I'm officially gone...maybe when they get older, you'll have the heart to tell them the real reason why.

This was not the time for him to walk away from me. Who was I going to lean on? Who was going to make me smile throughout the next six months that the doctor said I had left?

What I hope you get from this chapter is that, like it or not, obstacles are part of our lives. I had done so much self-work that I actually thought another trauma would never attack, but it did. My trauma still lingers today, but I was so mentally checked out that I totally disassociated from it. I went back for my PET scan results and was told the type and extent of my cancer. I was referred to the Cancer Center for further treatment, where I attended one appointment. From there on, I decided I would not go back. I did not have cancer. This was a joke. Someone would jump out at any moment and tell me it was all a big prank. No one did that, but it did not matter. I went back to work, deployed, and decided to suffer in silence. I did not tell a soul. I honestly thought that if I told no one about my cancer, it would go away. I believed this so much that I didn't even tell myself, not realizing that I was setting myself up for yet another long road to healing.

What now?

Here I am, six years after getting that six-month prognosis. I cannot tell you how long I stayed in bed after getting my diagnosis. I cannot even articulate how I pulled myself together, but I knew that I had to. I had little people—my children—who had no one else in the world to depend on but me. I had an entire platoon of people who depended on me. I had ten employees who depended on me. I had family members who depended on me. I wanted to shrink away so badly. The inability to come up with solutions messes with a person's mental state.

One day, I said to myself, "Self, you have got to find balance and implement some real positive thinking. If not, you are going to let this thing take you out." That is when it occurred to me that my mind, body, and spirit had to be balanced in order for me to really bring about lasting change in my life.

You must have control of your thoughts and always channel them towards what is good, wholesome, and positive. Your body must be treated as the temple that it is. It must be fed, watered, and tended to with as much devotion as any other living thing that human hands attempt to nurture, maintain, and preserve. Even while experiencing turmoil, you must learn how to find, accept, and embrace happiness, love, and forgiveness. Through this, you inevitably accept and embrace peace.

Cancer Revealed Some Ugly Truths.

Let me share something with you: The minute you get scared of cancer is the minute it starts to consume you. Cancer feeds on fear, and for a long while, I was filled with fear. I was filled with fear of missing out on my children's lives; fear of what cancer would do to my looks; fear of what people would think if they found out about my diagnosis; fear of losing the things that made me special; fear of never accomplishing any of my dreams; fear of there being nothing worthwhile, beautiful, or lovable left of me at the end of it all.

In order to find balance and reprogram to positive thinking, I had to work on channeling my mind into more positive things. Because cancer is as ominous an opponent as one could ever have, I could not be inconsistent with my positivity.

I decided that I would focus my time on figuring out the best way possible to live with, and hopefully get rid of, this ugly new best friend of mine.

I do not know anyone who could see cancer as a gift, yet it was through cancer that I received the greatest gift of true healing from past hurts and worries. My mindset has drastically changed. There are truths about myself that I would never have realized had cancer not forced me to discover them. I was able to heal from painful experiences that haunted me. I have been able to offer support to so many others who are battling this disease. I have discovered my true calling. It is ironic that all of this had to come at such great expense.

As tragic as my illness seemed, it led to a magical opportunity to change my life in ways I never thought possible. I have granted myself permission to create a completely new version of myself. My career, my lifestyle, and every other fundamental part of my life have taken on a new, exciting, and invigorating reality that I never would have considered before. I cannot control the journey, but I can always control how I experience the journey. By focusing on how I feel and on the people who I value in my life rather than what has happened to me, I am empowered. I am inspired each day to remain the architect of my own destiny.

I hope that sharing my story has helped you in some way and that it has at least given you food for thought. Whether you are journeying with cancer or watching a loved one struggle with it, I hope something here has moved you to be stronger, be braver, and have more understanding. I wish you health, I wish you happiness, and I wish you unending hope that your very best is still to come.

"My mission in life is not merely to survive, but to thrive, and to do it with some passion, some compassion, some humor, and some style."
— Maya Angelou

"Live in the present, for it is a gift….God takes care of our tomorrows."
— C Nicole Henderson

Chapter 4
Sai Lena Willis

Cracked but Never Broken

There was a lot about life that I already understood by the age of eleven—at least, I thought I understood. At this age, I quickly became more aware of the world around me and the reality that lay ahead. I explored the things that life has to offer and found myself living life in a fast lane and crying out in every way. I was misused as a child and had become numb to the fact that I was a victim, not knowing that a lot of young women had gone through the same things and had even committed suicide in some cases as a result of their traumas. When I was in the sixth grade, it all crashed down on me. I mean, that's when I began to snap my neck and twist my hips. I would always sit outside with hustlas like I was grown, demanding for a puff of a cigarette or a hit of a blunt. I would stand outside with some short shorts on, watching for the police to hit the block. Despite my young age, I was very mature mentally. I always had grown men in my face; there was something about the conversation I kept and the way I handled myself that always gave me a pass.

I can recall like yesterday the day I saw a boy on my block who was more than cute. I thought he was fine! I knew he was older than me, but I wanted to talk to him anyway. He seemed to also show interest in me. So, I always found my way outside when he came around. I always took the time to say hello and spark a conversation. I remember the day when he asked me how old I was. I turned around while swinging my hand back and forth across the gate.

"How old do I look?" I sharply replied. He looked at me, puzzled, and smiled as I held my head down.

"You look about fifteen."

"OK, then," I said as boldly as I could, knowing I was only eleven. Let's see what happens this time, I thought.

When I first laid down, I wasn't scared. Looking up at his eyes, I thought to myself, He's sixteen and he doesn't even know that I'm eleven. It wasn't long before someone found out and it got back to my mother that I was having sex, and that was the battle of all battles. I was being forced to remain the little girl who I no longer was while battling to be the young lady who I quickly became, and as a result of this, I began to seek love, attention, security, and affection from any man who would allow me the chance to receive it. However, it wasn't my fault; like so many other young women in society, I lacked real understanding. I did not understand how precious my innocence was, because as long as I can remember, someone had always been trying to steal the bit of innocence that I had. In the late 1990s, I went through a very challenging time. I couldn't even enter the eighth grade properly. I was already living in a group home, struggling to survive and figure out my way back home. Every day was a struggle as I tried to figure out who I was, where I was, and how to get back to what was familiar to me. Although it wasn't as strong as I wanted it to be, there was still some love at home.

I hated not being able to live life like a regular teenager and not having a fair chance at life. I was trapped in a sex-driven mindset, broken and bleeding from unhealed childhood scars as result of a molestation and mixed abuse. I wanted love, but didn't really know how to develop an ability to adapt to it nor willingness to accept it. I used to wonder all the time, Why don't I like these young boys?

Being able to just pick up my phone, call someone, and say, "Hey, I want this," or, "I want that," was so comforting to me. I was able to get what I wanted most of the time. See, I always surrounded myself with the kind of men who enriched me in one way or another, whether they helped in my everyday life, incorporated physical beauty into my lifestyle, or taught me something that was going to better me at some point.

I was watching a movie by myself one night when it became clear to me that I was just like almost every other woman. Women who started living adult lives at very young ages might not have been loved, protected, and guided properly. They might have been stripped of everything they were familiar with and were just trying to survive in the world. They might have been cracked, but never really broken—just like me. By the time I was eighteen, I had been with men who were well over ten years older than me. My child's father was three years older than me and my boyfriend was thirty-five. I went on to have multiple relationships with men who were between eight and twenty-five years older than me.

No matter if they were long-term or short-term arrangements, my relationships had stipulations. These relationships mostly required that I went to school, got good grades, and was the best on my team. When I upheld these standards, I was rewarded. I had a strong sense of survival, I was never homeless 'cause I always had what I needed and I never went without. For a long time in my life, I felt like a lost young girl. I had to keep a roof over my head and show someone that I was worthy of everything I wanted to do, but I didn't really know what I wanted to do. One day while listening to a lady speak on TV, I realized that I was not different from her, as if I was watching myself before my very eyes. I realized that I had been a sugar baby since the age of fourteen, although I had not known it before. It was very fun to me, and as I got older, the only men who interested me were the ones who were older than me. See, what made me different was that I was not only cute—I also had an outgoing personality.

Growing up in group homes, I had the benefit of learning a lot of etiquette skills that I was able to transfer over into my desired lifestyle. I learned how to walk and apply my makeup like a lady. I also learned how to eat at a table that was fully prepared. I learned exactly which glass to drink water from and which glass to drink wine from. I learned which fork was for my salad and which fork was for my dessert. I remember getting all dressed up and going to the nicest of restaurants in the city, where I would drink lovely red wine that complimented the best pieces of filet mignon the Bay Area had to offer. I would then enjoy a comedy show and some mind-blowing oral sex, then receive a handful of cash to get what I wanted when I went shopping with the girls. I did not realize that although I had everything I wanted, I did not have what I needed. I needed a chance to heal and to understand love, but since every form of love I had received thus far also came with a lesson, I learned to keep my walls up and guard my real feelings. Besides, the men I involved myself with were married, anyway. I wanted to be loved, but I didn't know how to receive love. For years, I thought I was in love because I endured abuse at the hands of those who said they loved me the most. I thought that in order to survive, I would have to use everything I had to get where I needed to go.

I used multiple websites in the past to find my sugar daddies because I was afraid to meet new people and I was never afraid to date online. Over time, I developed my sense of style and how I wanted to look on my profiles. I didn't want to look like a little girl, an escort, or a needy person. It was important for me to be mean and show myself, but not all of myself. See, I knew and understood that no one wants someone who shows everything upfront—I had to leave something to the imagination. Because I only dealt with married men, I never gave myself a chance to experience real love. The guys I dated outside of my sugar baby lifestyle were only infatuated with me.

When I relocated, I gave myself a chance at everything all over again. I decided that I was no longer going to repeat the same cycle. I was tired of feeling stuck and suffocated, like I could never find someone who was going to truly love me or support me. I just knew that I wanted more for my life and more for myself. I didn't see what I wanted around me, so I got on the Greyhound bus with my son and we left. For three days, I thought of how I was going to put myself in a better position. I was going to be the best version of myself possible. When I first moved, I wasn't thinking about a sugar daddy and I had started talking to a young man. Even at my new residence, I still seemed to have all the grown men turning their heads and smiling at me, even speaking to me. I went on a few unsuccessful dates and even had a few hookups. It wasn't long before I had a few men coming around, spending money on me, sending money to me, finding furniture for me, and making sure that my whole house was completely furnished.

One day, I remembered that I still had an active account on one of my website profiles. When I accessed my account, I realized that all I had to do was change my location. When I changed my location, oh, it was a whole new ball game. At this point in my life, I had my own place to stay and I had security at my job. I was not looking for a Captain Save-a-Hoe, but a real sugar daddy. I went on dates with a few idiots and had my time wasted. See, one of my main rules was always that my sugar daddy had to be married.

My rules made me feel protected. I didn't have to worry about anyone falling in love with me and I didn't have to worry about any attachments, which I thought was great because I had been detached from what love could feel like for so long. I never knew how it felt for someone to really love me, so to have an arrangement that was emotionally and sexually supreme but not completely there in terms of strings attached worked very well for me. I had opportunities to be with a few men who had millions of dollars, only to find out that they came with a lot of stipulations, because with money comes control. I think what made me stand out was the fact that I was uniquely honest about who I was and what I provided—what I liked and what I was looking for. I believe that for some sugar daddies, my profiles were very intimidating or I came across as high maintenance to them. But, hey, I had got rules and things that I stood by when it came to my sugar baby lifestyle.

One day, I came across a profile that was titled "Chivalry is Not Dead." I really can't remember if he saw me first or I saw him first, but our messages went back and forth. I saw his profile and thought to myself, You know, I'll give it a shot. I don't remember him looking anything like his profile photo in person. Although he used a real photo of himself, he still catfished me. Of course, just like I do with any other guy I meet on the internet, I asked my screening questions. I always want to know exactly who I'm talking to, so I ask personal questions when chatting with strangers online. We agreed to meet in person, and when we did, the vibe was right. We really enjoyed ourselves and he asked if I wanted to go home with him. I politely told him no, but that I would like to have breakfast with him in the morning, so we agreed to have breakfast the next day.

At breakfast the next morning, we discussed an arrangement and I got more information about his profile. He also gave me a chance to feel him out. We agreed to have a short-term arrangement that would allow us to see each other a few times a week. The allowances were pretty nice from the beginning and we just went from there. I never noticed that deep down inside, this man needed me just as much as I needed him. For the first few years, I showed him a side of me that no sugar daddy had really seen before because all of my sugar daddies before him were always married.

I fed him my home-cooked meals. I spent quality time with him, just chilling, watching movies, enjoying wine and cheese while cuddling on the sofa. On holidays when he was all alone, I would spend time with him and make sure he was fed. I didn't realize I was giving him everything he needed. I didn't realize he was the man I needed.

My sugar daddy would ask me if I would just be with him and stop being afraid to let my guard down. I would get upset and say no. I refused to let go of where I laid my head to follow behind a man who could just leave me and my son homeless. Hell, naw. I had to have my name on the deed or be married. He would beg me to let him help me raise my son and I would laugh, wondering why he would want to do that. He still showed me love and support.

Nevertheless, my sugar daddy paid for my classes and made sure I had everything I needed to pass. He supported all my goals and ideas. If I ever wanted to do something, I knew I had his full support. It was sweet. When he took me to Mexico and treated me like a queen, I knew that I was more than just arm candy to him and that I genuinely made him happy. I began to let myself be free. I passed my classes, and with his help, I was able to give back to my community and set up pathways for young girls. I started to open up and explain my wounds because I knew he could tell that I was not from Georgia and that I was very smart and determined to make it somewhere. I began to realize that I already had what I was praying for and that I needed to let go of what was holding me back.

One day, he looked into my eyes. "You act like you don't know what real love is because you don't even know when someone really loves you," he told me. Well, damn. He was right. I was tired of acting like I knew what real love felt like. All he wanted was someone real to spend his life with, and honestly, I wanted something real, too. Hell, I did not care about him being over thirty years older than me.

I was able to move my son out of the projects and get two degrees that landed me in successful business endeavors. My sugar daddy asked me to marry him and I said yes. I found someone who allowed me to heal mentally and emotionally. Some of us women go through some of the worst experiences in life and feel like there is no hope. I am asked all the time where I found my husband, and in a real but funny way, I say I found him on the internet.

Honestly, though, my husband was a godsend. I never had a man come into my life and say he would spoil me; provide for me; give me space, patience, freedom, love, and support; and want to help me raise my child. It was different from anything I was ever used to, and maybe for him, it took yet another shot at love to finally do it right because I definitely was not the first, second, or third woman he married. I spent years running from the beautiful young lady who I didn't know was inside of me, someone who everyone else with clear vision could see. I was blind, looking for love in fast lanes. Those lanes can get you killed.

Now, I'm married, and even though I've never had to do anything, I worked. When I was done working for other people, I looked at my husband and told him that I was ready to push my own businesses. He looked at me.

"Well, go ahead," he said.

I became a successful entrepreneur. I used my story in a way that helped me build a foundation to assist the next generation of young ladies who may feel broken inside. I established and opened Princess Tiona Foundation and Amercare Private Homecare Solutions, where I currently run everything independently. I have learned that in life, the experiences we go through are not meant to be kept to ourselves, but to be told as testimonies to give hope and encouragement to others. Over the years, I was treated for the molestation and abuse I experienced. I took the cards life handed me, played the game, and won.

"We may encounter many defeats, but we must not be defeated."
— Maya Angelou

Chapter 5
Jacqueline "Lulu" Brown

The Eccentric, Strong Black Woman:

The Good, The Bad, And the Ugly

Women show up with a pervasive and deep longing for something "more," but they can't always identify what that "more" is. We often tell every person of faith, sitting in anyone's church, that Jesus said, "Greater works shall we do." Women wait years to experience this great power God gives us.

Here is just one of many challenges: Very often, on the outside, you may have it all—the six-figure career, the house, the job, the kids, the husband, and all the luxury bags and shoes to match. However, you're struggling with feelings of "it" not being "enough." Maybe you are one of those women going through life with a constant heaviness in her heart and you beg for answers to the question, "Is this all there is?" Last, but certainly not least, you might have a truckload of challenges and issues that are not being addressed because you are going through the motions of being a woman of faith.

So, let's get to talking about why this is so important…

Here is how my journey started out:

I was given the name Jacqueline Lulu, but I'm fondly known as Lulu. I was named Lulu after the endearing and mischievous cartoon character, Little Lulu. I spent over thirty-eight years in Information Technology. During that time, I held technical, management, and executive leadership roles in Computer Operations, Telecommunications, Networks and Infrastructure, Call Center Technologies, Technical Support, Applications Development,

Software Quality Engineering, and Development Operations.

I thought I had balanced my career, world travel, and the execution of great ministry work, all while maintaining my position as one of many strong women in my family. Notice that I said, "I thought I had balanced" these things. I was not living my best life; rather, this was a life of reliving past hurts, being unhealed, living with a fight-or-flight mentality, dealing with self-worth issues, and… well, the list is too long, so let's go ahead and get to the meat of my story.

Here is the RAW truth: All my life, I was wearing a mask. I made a determination to become free and I did.

I am aware of masks and wearing them well. My life of wearing masks began on the day of my fifth birthday party. I was being raised by my wonderful great-aunt and her husband. I was given to them at about three months old. Both spent a great deal of time and effort to make my birthday party special. The setting was elegant for a five-year-old's party, with lace tablecloths, fancy china, crystal candy dishes, and a professional photographer. Adults and children were dressed "to the nines," as they say. My dad, grandmother, and sister looked exceptional for the photographer. There was one very important issue for me, however—my mother was missing. She said that she would be there, but on the day of my party, my aunt presented me with a beautiful dress from my mom and I was informed that she would not be at my party. My heart was broken and I suddenly didn't care if there was a party at all. I was reminded of how much effort was put into this elaborate party for me and how grateful I should be. I swallowed my heartache, put on a happy face, and remained joyful until that night when I cried myself to sleep. I didn't realize at the time that this was the beginning of my unsaid sentiments and my learned mask-wearing.

I learned at a very young age that there are some things one does not mention or talk about. We bury these things deep within; we harness them and control them to avoid them controlling us. As I approached adult life, all the unsaid things in my life began to manifest and I continued to hide them all behind my mask. I'd never witnessed any of the strong women in my family exhibit their true feelings or express what they were really going through at any given moment. I saw tough, strong, "put the better on the outside" type of behaviors. I normalized this and became an expert at mirroring what I saw in others. If it worked for them, it has to work for me, I thought.

Throughout my life, I often questioned my sanity, as I was intelligent enough to realize that I was suffering from a wave of unexpressed emotions that had manifested since my childhood. As I approached the age of fifty, I realized that the emotions behind my mask had to be uncovered, resolved, and killed at the root. I often felt frustrated, sad, isolated, weary, manipulated, shameful, depressed, hostile, used, overwhelmed, stressed, and like a failure.

I had little to NO self-worth. I married for the second time at age forty-two and brought a truckload of emotional pain and baggage into that union. I'd already experienced numerous mentally and physically abusive relationships before I reached the age of twenty-six.

I'd developed multiple personalities to fit any occasion. As an example, I demonstrated a type A personality to the maximum at work and in my career. Moreover, I could easily bounce back into my natural self, which is more of a type B, water-and-air personality.

As I took a harsh, honest look at myself, I realized that while I found great success in my career, business, and ministry work, I also felt the heavy burden of silently carrying my unsaid things. These unsaid challenges were never openly discussed as much as they should have been because of secret shame and, ultimately, the fear of revealing my true self. After all, I was Lulu, the crazy one! I was outrageous in my thinking; as a child, many thought I lived in a fantasy land because I thought differently, had a disdain for the status quo, and simply knew in my heart that my seemingly ridiculous dreams were attainable.

This incredible woman, Lulu, was everything to everyone. Yet, I felt the strain of my own mental, physical, and emotional neglect. I was giving to everyone else until there was nothing left for myself. I was quick to forgive others, but I was my own harshest critic. This was the model set for me and all the other women in my generation; however, I dare not speak such critical words about the elders from my grandmother's generation.

While holding strong in my position as one of many tough women in my family and thriving in my career, I learned that there is no such thing as balance, because all things can't always be treated equally. While I was deemed successful by society's standards, I knew in my heart that I hadn't reached my full potential. The barrier between me and my success was all that I had left unsaid. I had to break free from behind the mask. I'd show up in my professional career, dressed to the nines, on point, with presentations that knocked it out of the park and solutions to problems, often performing better than my peers, yet I was broken on the inside with my personal life in shambles. I remember there being bags of unopened mail on my table. Bills often went unpaid, even though I had enough money in my account to pay them. This held equally true in my spiritual life. I could minister to women on a level that was life-changing, but I remained lacking in many areas of my own spiritual life.

Let's not get it twisted—all that I've spoken of so far took place while I was a leader in the church, operating in several different capacities, yet still unhealed. While I made an awesome difference in the lives of others, I was perishing in my own life.

They say that when a person hits fifty years of age, something changes in their brain. This was very true for me. In 2010, I remember knowing and feeling my true calling and genius burning like fire shut up in my bones. I also knew that I was living a life of unresolved issues, pain, and untruths. Through self-discovery, reclaiming my own self-worth, and doing a lot of transformational healing and self-forgiveness work, I began showing up as my true self. Then, I realized that while I was successful in my career and my ministry work, I was enslaved in a religious matrix and certainly not walking in the total freedom and power that God desires for my life. Yes, you heard me… I said religious matrix.

I was ingrained in religious rules and regulations that had been handed down for generations, along with condemnation. From the ages of twenty to thirty-five, I was taught that my issues and lack of a breakthrough were because I was not going to church enough—I didn't make it to noonday prayer consistently, I was not attending church for every service and every pastor's appointment, and I was not putting God first in my life overall.

Everything was centered around not sinning versus being healed and whole from the inside out. The most important things were to be on time for church, clean the church on my assigned week, and usher on my assigned Sundays. Appearances became a major factor, even though that was not the intention of the leaders. This meant that no earrings, no pants, and no jeans should be worn because it was considered unbecoming of a saint. While slavery was not the intent, God's word was a yoke of condemnation and my ankles were chained.

My breakthrough started with prayer. Prayer was the one thing I learned that kept me going; it was and still is my greatest strength. I believe that prayer is part of my DNA, inherited from both of my grandmothers. It was also instilled in me by a great woman of God, my children's grandmother. Therefore, my conversations with God began to change. I began seeking God on a level that blew my own mind. I started to really hear God for myself. I started to apply God's word as a healing balm instead of a whipping stick. I dropped the chains, stepped into freedom, and began my own path to ascension in a radical and revolutionary way.

I set out on a path to grow beyond worldly and societal views of success. I sought professional help spiritually and mentally, and I began to change my business groups and social circles. I embraced my craziness, for therein was my genius. I removed naysayers from my ears. I became tone-deaf to anything that was contrary to my destiny. Through self-discovery, reclamation of my self-worth, and a lot of self-forgiveness work, I began showing up as my true self. I confronted every demon behind my mask, the biggest of which was self-denigration. I stopped allowing people to take my self-worth, which is something that many confuse with self-esteem. They are two different things and they manifest themselves differently in our lives for better or worse. I removed the worse and stepped into the better.

My recipe for becoming free was as follows: awakening, discovery, transformational healing, and ascension to my highest self.

Negative behaviors, such as emotional eating and living in constant fight-or-flight mode, were destroyed at the root and removed from my life. Confession, truth, and recovery were the stepping stones on my path forward. I set some major critical success goals for myself:

— Undergo a consciousness cleanse to connect with my soul's deepest purpose
— Kill Mammy; I am no longer the savior of everyone; that role belongs to Jesus
— Love myself as God loves me
— Walk in my brilliance
— Know my worth
— Embrace my craziness because it's my genius

After taking myself through a rigorous process, there were five key outcomes for me:

1. My self-worth grew by leaps and bounds as I took time to reflect on all the lives that God used me to change. My trips to India, the United Kingdom, France, Australia, Dubai, Israel, Spain, and many of the British islands allowed me to pour into other women and effect radical change in their lives. I was previously living in type A mode, where I never saw how God was using me and how valuable I was to others.

2. I now embrace my crazy, wild, and (sometimes) foolish imagination. Growing up, I was constantly called crazy, busy-bodied, loud, outrageous, confrontational, noisy, and disruptive. I was told that the things I believed to be possible were impossible. Over time, I allowed this message to diminish my outrageous dreams, but no longer. I've discovered that what some deemed as crazy was, and is, my genius.

3. I'm driven by love at a deeper, richer, and more ASCENDED level. My love for God, for myself, for my husband, for my family, and for great conversation became deeper and stronger. I developed a love for delicious, healthy food and broke the habit of emotional eating. Only the strength of love could have helped me to overcome the obstacles I've faced in my life. It inspires me, encourages me, and motivates me to continue spreading my God-inspired messages.

4. I believe that we, as women, are limitless. Here's the truth: There are no limits to our greatness. Our unsaid truths are holding us back. They form the gate which blocks our way; we simply need to look inside ourselves to find the key and unlock this gate.

5. My vibrational frequency became, and continues to be, energetic, dynamic, and uplifting. I'm a go-getter with a fire in my belly for praying, transforming lives, and making a meaningful impact in the lives of others. I'm also a great storyteller; I have the ability to share the lessons I've learned in order to help others.

Basically, I've grown leaps and bounds outside of my professional success, doing what God intended me to do, operating in my gifts, walking in my authentic self, and helping others to lose the chains of religious bondage and become the radical and revolutionary change themselves. This work energizes me, pulls me forward, and ignites my soul. This work is both my purpose and my legacy, and it's what I want to be remembered for most.

What the enemy meant for evil, God meant for MY GOOD…
In November of 2017, I was informed that I was being retired. This was divine intervention and it allowed me to shift my focus away from corporate America. Now, as a transformational speaker, women's empowerment consultant, and reverend/minister, I've spoken with and mentored women and young girls across the globe.

I host a weekly segment titled "Be Real Be Raw Be You with Lulu: The Lulu Experience" on iWorship96 FM radio. Additionally, I host a television segment on Blackhouse Media, streaming on the XOD platform. This anthology is the second book I've co-authored, and as a person who is naturally philanthropic, I serve as the Chairperson and Chief Program Officer for The Way Out Ministries, Inc., a 501c3 corporation.

Let's talk about my passion to start a revolutionary and radical movement required in today's church. I started out some years ago when I realized from experience that we are so ingrained in rituals such as wearing white to take communion and singing the hymns on cue that our gifts and powers are diminishing in the church.

Additionally, we've built the church house, but we've swept all of the garbage under the foundation. Here is what that means: People are having real issues and challenges. However, they come into a sanctuary one way and go back out the same way. In some cases, we've swept our own garbage under the foundation because we are not dealing with it. We often talk about how our grandmothers took us to church since we were babies and that we were raised in the church, yet as adults, we are often unhealed, living a lie, and simply going through the motions.

We quote scriptures that state, "Jesus said greater works will we do," but where are our greater works and what are those greater works? Why do we have such a high divorce rate in our religious institutions? Why does sexual harassment take place in our religious institutions? Is it because the church has become just that, an institution, and is no longer a safe place for refuge and help in dealing with our challenges and issues—a real solutions sanctuary?

As I asked myself these questions and took a hard look at where we are as people, I went deeper and asked myself, Are my values and motivation aligned with my purpose? Are my purpose and values in alignment with each other? I saw that there was more work to do within myself and with others.

I realized that if we are to really do greater works as Jesus stated, we must operate from a greater seat of power, a place of miracles. We must possess a mindset in which we know who we are and what God says we are, and that we have the power. We must begin to position ourselves to receive this power, which is exactly what I did on a new level.

Next, I dug deeper and asked myself, Are we being true to ourselves and speaking our truths—our unsaid truths—or are we still holding back?

The more I took myself through this process of elevation, I realized that there was more for me to complete within myself and to teach to others. There is a deeper level of getting to the root of the matter and speaking our unsaid truths—those things that we don't talk about, but need to talk about.

There is an essential concept that we understand: Women at every level are divinely created to be strong leaders and bring essential skills, strategic thinking, and divine feminine acumen to their roles. To flourish as a leader, a woman needs not only the skills to lead, but also a dynamic voice that can be heard and followed. First, though, we need to discuss our unsaid truths and discover the root of the issues within our own lives, and there must be a safe space for us to do so. The path and process I was creating got deeper. There were additional areas for me to cover:

1. Do we know who we are? This focus shifts into leading others and presenting oneself as someone who adds value to any given space. Knowledge of who we are as women, the stolen history of ancient Egypt, and how we move forward are essentials to removing the cycle of religious enslavement in our lives.

2. Freedom from enslavement, coming from behind the masks we wear to church like our Sunday best hats. We say that we are born-again Christians, but are we truly in a place of rebirth? Mammy or Matriarch? We must master ourselves before we try to save the world.

3. Church folks, often women, can easily become enslaved noisemakers without power. Rituals don't help us to operate from a seat of power. We must define the purpose of our praise.

4. Can we come from behind our Sunday best masks, live true and authentic lives where our spirits are truly aligned to all that we do, and operate from a true place of rebirth? We must become our own masters and become empowered to help others.

God gives us marvelous talents and gifts. It took years for me to appreciate my uniqueness and the power that resides within.

I always knew, in the deepest part of my heart, that I was destined for greatness; however, I never spoke the words aloud. I certainly didn't envision that I would carry an unpopular, yet necessary message to masses of women. I didn't envision that I would equip others with the ability to reach their highest elevation. More importantly, I didn't know that such a calling would come with major transformation and healing. My divine calling required my willingness to hear the truth and go through my own process of awakening, discovering myself, reclaiming my self-worth, forgiving myself, identifying my genius, operating in my authentic self, and allowing God to order my footsteps.

As the years went by, I grew in ministry. I love doing anything that involves the empowerment of women. I often make mistakes, but now, I persevere instead of giving up. I continuously study and receive wisdom, knowledge, and a better understanding of my life's purpose.

God's revelation showed me the need to transform the lives of women and help them come from behind their masks.

I once knew this mask all too well and broke through it. I saw and accepted the assignment to revolutionize our Black churches by designing programs which address the unique needs of women from a God-centered perspective of freedom, rather than keep these women in the chains that currently enslave us under the disguise of godliness.

Many people are not walking in their God-given superpowers. Who they are is not in divine alignment with their spirit.

As people of God, we speak clichés such as "The sky's the limit" when God has given us power, authority, and dominion over all things. There is no sky and there are no limits besides the ones that we create for ourselves.

I now provide a radical approach to addressing the needs of women who are seeking their purpose. We must lead and minister with new insights about our feminine power, our divine gifts, and how to make radical positive change in the lives of others. I am an eccentric, strong Black woman who survived the good, the bad, and the ugly, and I know that every woman deserves a bright, shining life that sings to their soul. I've unmasked my voice and God has given me a message to spread to all women. Now, hear me ROAR!

"Power and greatness were in me from when I was in my Mother's womb; the enemy is unable to stop God's divine purpose and destiny for my life".
— JLB, The Lulu Experience

"To 'TRY' is To Resist Yourself." — C Nicole Henderson

Chapter 6
Chanel Nicole Ryan

"You are not the first woman to get pushed."

These words were jarring, like a knife with a jagged edge. Hearing these words as the response to my disclosure that a domestic violence incident had recently taken place was devastating. The first time I heard these words, they were spoken during the first of two phone calls I made in the middle of the night as I was seeking help for myself following a domestic violence incident. What was especially hurtful was hearing these words spoken from the lips of a family member. I can remember my initial shock and the immediate numbness that followed. These words cut so deep that it became dangerous to feel in that moment. But whether I could sense it or not, these words immediately assaulted my psyche and began circulating as unchecked trauma within my body. But despite how painful it was to hear these words, these same words were the catalyst that caused me to embark on a significant journey to recovery.

In Recovery

Disappointment held me down
and fenced me in,
swallowing my hopes for a season.
I traveled a road watered with tears
and drank from a stream of longing.
I sat at its bank,
trying to make sense of chaos,
collecting my thoughts.
My heart stabilized, bypassing pain
through open creative channels.
I lie in recovery gaining strength—

One step closer to moving forward.

"You are not the first woman [in your family] to get pushed."

An interesting image lay before me: a diagram filled with squares, circles, and linking lines representing the various generations within my family lineage. One of my assignments during my training to become a certified trauma recovery coach involved the completion of a genogram spanning at least three generations. A genogram resembles a family tree; both documents begin with generational organization of family members. However, the genogram I was asked to create involved more than simply tracking my family lineage. Its purpose was to capture and highlight familial and generational trauma.

My finished genogram revealed a consistent and glaring pattern, specifically within my maternal lineage. Every woman listed for three generations, including myself (please note that this was not an all-encompassing list of every woman in my maternal lineage), had experienced some form of abuse: sexual abuse, child abuse, and/or domestic violence. If I had been tracking the progression of a disease, I would have labeled this pattern a familial pathology. Needless to say, I was shocked and rendered speechless by the generational trauma within my own family. Over the years, I had been exposed to scattered, fragmented, and whispered stories that individually held little meaning for me. But collectively, those same stories, despite being incomplete, connected three generations of women along a jagged red line of abuse. After seeing this familial pattern, I began to reframe the context of those haunting words. "You are not the first woman to get pushed" became "You are not the first woman in your family to get pushed."

Maybe if Brown

became black and blue,
or if words could leave a visible mark,
I would have given the situation a better name.
Instead, I rationalized,
suppressed, and denied, not knowing that
a better reality awaited me.

I died a slow and painful death,
just like an oak
strangled by mistletoe.

The truth was that the bodies and minds of the women in my family had been assaulted for generations. I was one of many. Seeing and understanding this larger and extended pattern caused mixed feelings for me. There was shock and sadness, hurt and grief, and then a sudden curiosity. Previously, the words, "You are not the first woman to get pushed" had only been a source of significant pain and confusion. However, when placed in the larger context of my generational traumatic history, I saw that those same words held an entirely different meaning. This dangerous pathology of abuse had been passed down through generations unchecked, and silence and secrecy invited the pattern to continue. In this moment, a question loomed before me: Who did I want to be? I had a choice: I, too, could fall silent, or I could choose to do something entirely different. I could choose to start talking; I could choose to allow those words to push me to continue seeking answers; I could choose to break the cycle.

Those initially hurtful words became the catalyst that unleashed not only my personal healing, but also the healing of generations of women. They were the first clue that exposed the full scope of the generational abuse that had taken place within my family. I may never know how many women before me heard those words or how those words affected them. What I do know is that I am the first woman in three generations to have the courage to publicly document them and truthfully share my response to them.

Speaking Spirit

Left among the thorns,
beauty began to fade,
retreating deeper within.

Great were the crimes
committed against her land,
but in silence
a greater injustice occurred—
her voice failed to cry out.

Justice demands
that she speak.

I chose speech instead of silence, but there are risks associated with truth-telling. Often, there are toxic relational and familial systems whose foundations are fortified by secrecy and silence. Truth-telling significantly threatens the stability of those structures. The choice to be a cycle-breaker disrupted my entire world. No relationship in my life was unaffected. Truth-telling was a polarizing act that divided the people in my life into two camps: those who were sincerely for me and those who were not. There was absolutely no middle ground. For the first time, I knew where I stood with every person in my life. It was shocking to see where the dividing line fell. I lost significant relationships swiftly and painfully, but I was also simultaneously strengthened in the midst of these losses; they created space in my life for healthier relationships. In hindsight, it was a very powerful state to be in. Truth-telling, while disruptive and painful, ushered in a tremendous amount of healing and transformation.

Would it have been easier to just keep quiet and maintain the peace? Perhaps. I could have chosen to continue the legacy of the jagged red line and left the work to the next generation—but at what cost? I would have to betray myself. Instead, I consciously chose to do the hard work right then, even if it cost me relationships. Some view my decision to honor myself as a personal betrayal, but when left with the choice to dishonor myself by remaining silent or to honor myself by speaking, I choose to speak and let the chips fall where they may.

Breaking the Silence

Abuse buried in silence kills,
murdering the spirit of the victim
while enabling
the crime of the offender.

Help comes from disclosure:
the held captive set free
with vitality renewed and restored,
walking in victory.

The jagged red line also represents a generational pattern of silence and self-betrayal. I grew up in a familial culture of secrecy and silence. I suspect that, for many of the women who came before me, silence started as a survival technique. Throughout the generations, however, that same silence became toxic. Silence limited my ability to thrive. I could not operate in health and remain silent. Silence was too destructive to my spirit. I honor myself and the women who came before me by giving them voice and expressing what they could not or would not say.

In 2011, I wrote and self-published a book titled *Things Said*. It was a collection of poetry and a high-level attempt to speak about my personal experiences with abuse. I recently made the decision to revise and expand this body of work because I failed to claim the story as my own. I filled this publication with images, which gave the impression that the story I was sharing belonged to someone else. I recognize now that I was still hiding. In the expanded and revised edition, I made it very clear that the story I told was my own. This was not someone else's story. The experiences documented happened to me and the responses chosen were mine.

It's a powerful thing to tell the ugly and painful parts of a story. Oftentimes, people omit those parts because they are usually laced with profound shame. However, once I was courageous enough to move beyond the shame, I discovered that the once ugly and painful parts were moments of commonality and connection. I spent the last several months training to become a certified trauma recovery coach. Much of that training consisted of sharing my story with other trauma survivors and learning to create and hold space for others to do the same.

A key component for truth-telling, whether for ourselves or others, is safety. I believe that when people feel safe, this safety creates the necessary space for truth to emerge. In my trauma recovery journey, I had to accept some hard truths and commit to telling myself the truth while simultaneously learning how to share that truth safely with others. The "safely with others" part is very important. It is very difficult to give voice to the truth without a safe space to do so in. Growing up in a familial culture of secrecy and silence did not teach me or provide me with an avenue of safety. Consequently, employing the methods I learned from that faulty system did not facilitate a pathway to health or healing. Trauma and abuse don't heal in an environment of secrecy and silence; under those conditions, they are simply transferred. A huge shift in my healing journey happened when I discovered and began to participate in a culture of safety separate from my family of origin. It allowed me to witness and experience safety and begin cultivating that same safety within myself. Furthermore, in cultivating safety for myself and with others, I am better equipped to give others the space and freedom to do the same. It is my sincere pleasure to continue my journey of liberation by walking alongside others as they travel the same path.

The truth is, I am NOT the first woman to get pushed. I am not the first woman in my lineage or the first woman globally to be impacted by abuse. What I am is a woman who is willing to honor herself while holding space for others who choose to do the same.

Flourishing Palm

I am a woman,
Splendid queen of influence.
My hands change the world.

A Queen's Ensemble: "We were all created with unique gifts given by God. This means that to be created in His image makes us perfect, complete, and lacking nothing. To think we can be perfection alone creates an unsound mind. To know we are perfected through community in lifting one another empowers an ensemble."

— Conswella Smith

"Do the best you can until you know better. Then, when you know better, do better."
— Maya Angelou

Chapter 7
Toyin Fadina

There is No Mountain High Enough:
A Strong Black Woman Story

"Through the strong Black woman stigma, Black women have been conditioned to believe that they are supposed to accept . . . the [oppression] that confronts them, all while taking care of their families with little to no support."
— Tanisha Nicole Stanford, "African American grandmothers as the Black matriarch: you don't live for yourself."

As strong Black women, we are conditioned to believe that there are no limits to what we can take on. We are conditioned to handle everything perfectly in our homes, workplaces, and communities. Hence, a strong Black woman typically takes on leading roles with countless expectations and responsibilities that lead her to neglect her own well-being, failing to realize that everyone has a limit. Self-care is important.

When it was time to step into the role of a strong Black woman, I was already numb to pain and ready for anything thrown my way. I was accustomed to carrying immense weight on my shoulders and not showing it.

Following generations of systemic racism and setbacks, mountains have always been tough to climb for Black women. It's unfortunate that even those who have "made it" as leading Black women struggle with similar setbacks. Much remains unchanged in 2020, when influential Black women like Oprah Winfrey, Viola Davis, Stacy Abrams, Michelle Obama, and Kamala Harris undergo the same pain as I do. I believed it was our birthright as Black women to wear huge letter Ss on our chests because we were everyone's she-roes. My mountains were similar to the ones other women had to climb in order to obtain equality, freedom, and the "good life" for their families.

In December 2020, although the world was amidst a pandemic, I was not bothered. Why? Because I was a strong Black woman. I could take on anything—at least, I thought I could—until I reached my limit. I spent so much time working that I rarely saw daylight. Soon, I experienced unusual pains throughout my body, with my head feeling like it had been hit by a train. I was short of breath and experiencing chest palpitations. This is impossible for me, I thought. Besides having asthma, I rarely get sick. So, I kept working through my daily activities until I found myself crying uncontrollably. This was greater than an asthma attack—it was an anxiety attack!

Looking around the room, I wondered, How did I get here? Why is my body in so much pain? I finally heard my body shouting, "I'm hurt!" I had a sharp pain in my abdomen and could feel all of my muscles tightening. I needed more than an inhaler and Tylenol. I was afraid to go to the emergency room because I knew I did not have COVID-19 and didn't want to put myself at risk, as the hospitals were crowded with COVID-19 patients. I felt safer staying home alone, and I thought I would feel better in the morning. I was more concerned about not missing work the next day than about my health.

That night, I was afraid to go to sleep because my blood pressure was unusually high and the pains traveling from head to toe were becoming unbearable. My eyes twitched and my vision was blurry. I was too weak and dizzy to walk around and I knew that high blood pressure could be a silent killer or lead to other health issues. Was I having a stroke or a heart attack? I realized that I was at my breaking point. I was embarrassed; I had taken on the belief that a strong Black woman like myself was unbreakable. I had been through being broke, homeless, a single parent, and betrayed. Why am I breaking now? I pondered. I am an empty nester with a degree, a good job, a smart child, and a great living situation. Why am I breaking down after all I have been through? I thought I was living the good life.

After I prayed, I felt like the walls were closing in on me. I swallowed my pride and called a friend to help me. I was at odds with myself and I had to teach my students without displaying any trace of what I had gone through. A close friend of mine understood that I thought my identity revolved around being a teacher; she counseled me to remember myself.

She reminded me that I had other hidden gifts and talents that were needed in this world and in my career. She asked me to go find a mirror and to recite her words. I thought it was ridiculous and refused to do it until she shouted at me.

"Repeat after me," she said.

"Okaaaay," I replied in a reluctant voice.

"Are you looking in the mirror?" she asked me.

"Yes," I said, irritated.

"Say, 'My name is Toyin, and I have one child,'" she ordered.

She could hear my frustration. I could not believe she was making me play games at the most detrimental point in my life. I had never called a friend crying for help.

"Say it again, louder: 'My name is Toyin, and I have one child,'" she yelled.

I did as she said. At this point, I thought I had made a mistake by calling her.

"If you do not take care of yourself, you do not have to worry about not returning to work because you will not be alive," she continued.

A lightbulb shone in my head. I knew she was right because I had been living for work and I was now suffering from burnout because of it. I did not feel as if I was truly living. I knew I had to change. I was determined to start saying no to others in order to say YES to myself.

How Did I Get Here?

It was not unusual for me to feel emotionally, mentally, and physically sick during the nights after or mornings of my classes. I would experience anxiety from the overload of work and expectations. My weight fluctuated due to binge eating and I gained nearly twenty pounds within two months of teaching virtually. I was distraught because I had gained back all of the weight that took six months to shed. There was so much anxiety around returning to work during a pandemic after a summer of protests and rallies surrounding George Floyd, Breonna Taylor, Black Lives Matter, and Donald Trump. I was emotional over the COVID-19-related deaths of family members and close friends, as well as many historic leaders, such as John Lewis, C.T. Vivian, and Ruth Bader Ginsburg. The pain of these losses mounted on top of preexisting pressures in the field of education, where teachers are expected to reach unattainable goals with inadequate tools, resources, or support. I was returning to work without a clue what to expect because the school system I worked for was indecisive about many prudent issues that impacted me directly. Because I had an underlying health condition during a pandemic, I did not know if I would have a job or not. How was I going to make it as a single mom trying to put my child through college?

In October of 2020, there were no clear answers about what accommodations to expect. The school district was very indecisive about returning to the classroom and tensions in the field of education heightened. I was emotionally impacted by the number of teachers who were experiencing major health issues, getting cancer, or dying. I was trapped in a whirlwind of fears. On top of that, I had to perform a balancing act of testing and teaching. I was disturbed by the number of tests we had to administer virtually. I felt terrible; it seemed like we were testing our students more than we were teaching them.

I was shocked by the miracles and humanly impossible tasks we were expected to perform during the pandemic. Although I was competent to teach virtually, I was torn; I did not have the resources, tools, and support I needed in order to deliver the high-quality education I was accustomed to providing for my students.

There came a point where I could not function throughout my typical daily activities or even step outside of my home because I had become so busy working in my new virtual environment. For the first time in my life, I stayed indoors for seven days straight. I did not realize that I had spent seven days in my home without feeling sunlight on my skin. This is quite scary, I thought. This was more than a pandemic causing me to feel restricted in my home. I was clinically depressed. I can only remember thinking to myself, I've devoted the last fifteen years to my career and to working around the clock. Don't get me wrong—I love impacting young minds through my work. However, I had reached my limit, as I was moving through a life I did not truly feel alive in.

I feared that I would not get another teaching job. I felt like I was incapable of becoming a strong Black woman again. I realized that my self-worth was wrapped up in my career and that my confidence was spiraling. This created more anxiety within me, which I knew could lead to more serious health issues. I could not work another day under those conditions.

It might sound absurd now, but I thought that I would never get hired again due to the fact that I had a mental breakdown during the pandemic. It broke my heart to leave my students, but I knew that I had to care for my health. I felt like I was in an unwinnable situation. If I returned to work, I would risk having a stroke or heart attack; if I left my students in the middle of the school year, I would experience heartache.

I knew people would make derisive comments about me leaving work to care for my health, but I could not care about that. I put into practice the directions given to passengers before a plane takes flight: Put the oxygen mask over your own face before saving others. In the words of my late great Aunt Doll, "You've got to save yourself first, babe."

I worried about my financial status, health, and job so much that anytime I reflected on my situation, my anxiety was triggered.

Healing Begins

Due to work, I experienced burnout, hopelessness, depression, and humiliation. I reached my breaking point. I felt vulnerable to criticism from everyone around me for speaking my truth. Today, I am much better. When the stress began to take a toll on me, I knew I had to discover what contributed to the weight on my shoulders. I had to remove the root causes of my stress. My experiences had a greater impact on me than I originally thought they did. I discovered that this was the result of me never saying no to others. I thought that I could do it all.

I realized that I could not care for anyone else until I cared for myself first. I had helped so many people through my career and community service efforts, but I could not help anyone else until I took the steps to help myself first.

The next day, I did not report to work. I decided to take a medical leave and care for myself. I took a hiatus from all white noise, including loved ones, to reset, revive, refresh, and restore my mind, body, and spirit. I began a two-step total health process, which forced me to cleanse and revitalize myself

in order to heal. I had to cleanse myself by identifying and eliminating toxic situations and the factors that contributed to them. I cleansed my body of behaviors, people, and situations that were unhealthy. I took a break from people, social media, and the news and began to revitalize myself. Many of my friends and family members thought I was insane, but I had to restore myself with positive energy. I found the perfect counselor and invested in coaches who helped me pivot onto a journey toward healthy living. I was doing the impossible—I was turning my life around.

For years, I was numb to the pains that my body experienced because I had refused to listen to what my body was telling me—many years of saying no to myself and yes to everyone else had built up and I was now dealing with the resulting damage. I was tired and torn up inside. I had been carrying the burdens and troubles of everyone but myself. While it took a pandemic for me to truly reach my breaking point, I had already been breaking down for years. The pandemic was simply the straw that broke the camel's back. Now, I was forced to do something that I had never done before. I did not have a clue where to go for help or how to care for myself. This is not what I do. I care for others, not myself, I thought. How was I going to climb the giant mountain of dealing with myself?

I was in disbelief that I could climb this mountain until I experienced a flashback of my childhood with my grandmother, with whom I lived off and on throughout my early life.

The first mountain I ever had to climb was learning how to live with the family's matriarch—my grandmother, Mrs. Rosie Mae Oliver. There is a joke that says that if a person's middle name is Mae, they are not one to mess with. I would love to tell you that my grandmother was a sweet old lady who passed out cookies, but that was not the case.

She was a loving woman who passed out housework, butt whoopings, and life lessons. Everyone knew that you did not challenge Rosie Mae. Of course, I tested the waters and discovered her strength the hard way. After spending most of my life with such a strong woman, I later realized why she was so strict and came to appreciate all of the lessons I learned from her.

I often reminisce about our moments together and how she taught me to never give up. In 2020, when I was facing one of the largest mountains I ever had to climb, I knew that I could do it, thanks to my grandmother. She taught me how to press through hard times, as she had experienced devastating moments of her own—from watching loved ones and every leading man in her life killed to devoting her entire life to loving, raising, and protecting others. During the Jim Crow era, she endured hurt, anxiety, fear, humiliation, and shame. Through it all, she managed to raise her siblings, children, and grandchildren with limited resources and support.

She knew how to make a way out of no way. I cannot imagine climbing the mountains that my grandmother faced in her life, but due to her example, I knew that I could get through my personal situation during the pandemic. My grandmother made the mountains of my life look like hills to climb. God will never give you more than you can handle.

Who Am I Today?

The song "Ain't No Mountain High Enough" reminds me that no barriers or obstacles will stand in my way. From childhood to adulthood, I climbed mountains of darkness, despair, heartache, disappointment, and defeat. I know that I can reach the top of any mountain and claim my victory. From all the leading women in my life, I learned that the real secret to climbing any mountain is to use your life's GPS (God's Positioning System) and allow God to direct your life by remembering to "seek God's will in all that you do . . . He will direct your path" (Proverbs 3:6).

Now, I am at the greatest point in my life. I now see daylight regularly and I make time for walks. I no longer have to take as many medications. I am living a more balanced life after taking the necessary time to focus on my mind, body, and spirit. I make time for myself, even when it seems impossible to do so. I read daily devotional passages to keep my spirits lifted. Recently, I lost fifty pounds through healthy eating and exercise. I practiced the mindful habit of pouring only from a full cup, and I never let my plate get full. I focus more on self-care and self-enrichment; I plan and organize my life so that I don't become overwhelmed. I practice spiritual meditation and yoga, which I learned from my daughter. Mostly, I practice the art of saying no. I put myself first. If something does not make me happy, I do not make space for it in my life. I make sure that I care for myself just as much as I care for others. I finally have a balanced life and am able to live out my purpose. I only welcome things into my life that bring me joy.

The ultimate lesson I learned was that my breaking point was actually my breakthrough—God showed me that. Everything you go through is for your own good. My setback made me stronger than I ever was before.

What Do I Do for Others Now?

I look at myself differently now. I realized that we all go through painful moments, but what matters is whether or not we choose to do something about these moments. I am sharing my story, hoping that I inspire others to climb the seemingly unconquerable mountain of dealing with themselves by choosing to transform their lives.

I truly care about people and what they experience in their lives. I empathize with people because I share similar experiences and I use my story to help others break the silence that their depression has caused. I motivate them to walk in their truths and to live fulfilling, healthy, and happy lives by any means necessary. I encourage them to be courageous enough to transform into the best versions of themselves and to never give up.

Dear Sis,

I wrote this chapter to inspire and challenge you—a woman of any race, lifestyle, or belief system—to start your self-care journey by standing in your truth and making your happiness nonnegotiable. Start by getting prudent about everything you are involved in; become laser-focused on your desires. Someone once said, "If it does not make you happy, simply do not do it." When things get challenging, use the K.I.S.S. method: Keep It Simple, Sis! Do not make life more complicated than it has to be. Let go of other people's baggage and focus on your journey. Say no to things that do not fit into your life. God has a great future for you, and it is time to live out God's divine plan
and heal yourself by letting your light shine. It is never too late to say yes to loving yourself.

Gracefully find balance, peace, and happiness in a world of chaos; be your own muse. Just learn to let go and let God! Choose to cross out the S on your chest instead of constantly trying to be everyone's she-ro. I said yes to myself. Will you say yes to yourself, too, and join me on a new, smart wellness journey?

The SMART Life

A quote that I faithfully live by is, "All it takes is faith the size of a mustard seed to move mountains." The mountain I faced in late 2020 seemed to be a giant one, but I was ready to face it head-on until I reached the top, thanks to my late grandmother and her life lessons on how to never give up. She taught me to give my troubles to God.

I now have a smart, balanced life in which I serve God, myself, and others in exactly that order. I no longer pour from an empty cup and run around with my full plate toppling over. I am no longer afraid of saying no to others because I enjoy saying yes to loving myself. I am in a good place with my new relationships, lifestyle, career, and business.

It feels good to know that my mental breakdown was actually a breakthrough. It was a moment that allowed me to reset my life in order to heal myself and others through my new self-enrichment strategies. I can truly connect with, understand, and empathize with all women who tell me their stories. I advocate for them and their children the best way I know how through my S.M.A.R.T, Inc. nonprofit organization. I once feared living out my purpose, but I am now courageous enough to have the audacity to let my light shine.

Toyin Fadina

Matthew 5:16 says, "Let your light so shine before men, that they may see your good works, and glorify your Father which is in heaven." KJ21

"Wrote this book to support you." — Billionaire PA

Chapter 8
April Sanders

I ESCAPED

No, I wasn't born in April, but my mother was! She thought that April was a perfect name for the beautiful baby girl she gave birth to on the morning of Thanksgiving Eve. She gave me Lynn as a middle name; this was the name of my aunt, who was also my Godmother.

At the age of seventeen, my mother was prescribed medication for mental health complications. She found out that she was pregnant with me at the age of twenty-two; the duration of her pregnancy would be the only time she was able to manage without medication. Three months after giving birth to me, my mother suffered another nervous breakdown, which caused her to never be able to raise and tend to her one and only child.

My grandmother took custody of me despite the doubts of family members who told her that she should not let my mom give birth to me. The story I was told is as follows: all of the family members met up at my grandmother's house with the intention of changing my grandmother's mind. They asked questions like, "How are you going to take care of her and a baby?" and made statements like, "You know she can't take care of a baby" and "You shouldn't let her have it."

"Debbie is going to have this baby! I took care of the rest of them, and some of yours, too! Whoever don't like it can get the fuck out of my house!" she yelled with tears in her eyes. She was a feisty, cursing lady. My grandmother, hurt and disgusted with everyone, went outside.

"Mickey, how are you going to take care of Debbie and the baby?" they asked her again.

"WATCH ME!" she shouted as she walked out.

Months later, I was born, and my grandmother was committed and driven to do whatever she could to help me fulfill my destiny. She never considered the real value of the way she cared for me with all the chaos that surrounded us.

You see, not only was my mother diagnosed with bipolar disorder, schizophrenia, and manic depression; it was the history behind the mental illnesses that led to the diagnoses. My mother grew up in an abusive home, where she witnessed and experienced mental, physical, emotional, sexual, and substance abuse from her father toward her, her mother, and her siblings. That, of course, led to some severe emotional difficulties. At the age of sixteen, somebody laced my mother's drink and joint of marijuana with angel dust while she was at a party and she was gang raped by a group of men. So, by seventeen, she suffered a nervous breakdown and was never the same.

I experienced most of my childhood visiting my mother in a state psychiatric hospital. As a child, I never understood why my mother had to be there. When I visited her, she wasn't like the other individuals surrounding her. I hated that place; it had the worst smell and the people would walk around muttering to themselves. My mother did not stink, nor did she mutter to herself; instead, she would enter the visiting area looking and acting her best. She was normal to me.

Home was my second least favorite place to be. Although my grandmother had already divorced my grandfather before I was born, all of her children still resided with us and, of course, had their own damage from the chaos they witnessed growing up. The verbal, physical, and substance abuse were all still present. Although my grandmother would always keep me close to her, I still witnessed it all. Those were some of the most painful times. I was always embarrassed and ashamed, and my self-worth and self-esteem were snatched away from me. I always wanted to escape. I didn't want to be there.

My mother lived a life of dual residence, spending half a year in the hospital and the other half at home with us. When she was home, she mainly abused crack cocaine and alcohol. She was very stubborn and never listened to anyone, especially my grandmother. She knew it all; she chose to do only what she thought was best. I remember a time when my mother tried to sneak one of her boyfriends into the house through the back door. I happened to come into the kitchen while she was doing this. She was also trying to get one of the spoons that I hated to use because they were always black and burnt at the bottom. Shocked that I was in the kitchen and afraid that I would tell my grandmother, because I did tell on all of her siblings, she looked at me with her eyes as wide as a car's high beams.

"I will kill you, bitch! Get out of here!" she shouted at me.

I just stared at her. That was the worst pain I had ever felt. As my eyes filled up with tears, I ran and told my grandmother what had just happened. Let's just say that was the last night I saw my mother at home for a very long time. She immediately went back to her other residence.

Until I was about six or seven years old, I would always get a visitor at the house who only I could see. To me, he looked to me like a man with a shadow face. He would just stand in the hallway of my home and stare at me. He would watch everything I did. I wasn't scared, but I would tell my grandmother, "The man is staring at me again!" She would tell me to tell him to go away. I would yell, "Go away! Leave me alone!" Then, he would flee. Once I started attending church consistently at around the age of eight, I never saw him in my home again.

After attending church for a couple of years, at the age of ten, I accepted Jesus as my Lord and Savior. I felt safe away from home and usually spent most of my time with three of my girl cousins who were all sisters. We all referred to them as "the girls," and until about the age of thirteen, I was considered their fourth sibling. They were my best friends. I enjoyed spending time with them. I felt free; being a kid was easy. I loved school, and in the fourth and fifth grades, I had amazing teachers who saw my potential and gave me tools. They told me, "Never rest until your better is BEST," and taught me that excuses would make me incompetent. Leadership came naturally to me and I always wanted the best for myself and those who surrounded me, even my family members. I wanted all of them to be better and do their best, but I was looked at as if I knew it all and as if I felt I was better than them.

Once I started going through the most critical time of adolescence, all of the anxiety and trauma I experienced at a young age came upon me. I did not feel like a kid anymore and I didn't want to be around "the girls" anymore. I felt things that I could not explain, and although I no longer saw the man who watched me as a child, I always had weird experiences relating to things that I knew were going to happen. I felt things and would never mention them to anyone. On top of the pain of not having parents, especially a father, all of the chaos started to build up inside of me and I just couldn't talk to anyone. I didn't want to sound crazy. I didn't want to be like my mother.

By the age of sixteen, I was pregnant, and my life took a turn that I never saw coming. I decided to have my child. I wanted so badly not to be a statistic and repeat a cycle that everyone assumed I would perpetuate. I told my high school vice principal about my pregnancy because I missed detention and she didn't play that.

"Oh, honey, your life is over! I feel sorry for you. I don't understand why you young girls get caught up and make stupid decisions." She was the first person to tell me that my decision was not the best, and she certainly wasn't the last. Even when I was finishing up my second trimester, people were still trying to encourage me not to keep my child.

I couldn't believe it. It made me sad and I wanted to get away from everything that held me down. I wanted to prove her and everyone else who doubted me wrong, so I went to college. I started a career and I did everything I could so that my daughter and I would have a better life than expected. I thought that doing the right thing would set me free. I thought that the pain and trauma from my past experiences with my family would go away if I just forgot about them, kept them inside, and kept moving forward. I was always searching for a way to escape. Whether my escapes included men, alcohol, or social activities, I just needed to get away. None of my distractions really worked, and one day, everything built up and I broke. I just couldn't believe it. I didn't break free, but I broke, just like my mother. At the age of twenty-eight, I found myself in a mental institution similar to the one where I would visit my mother during my childhood.

I just could not believe that after trying so hard to hold myself together, I was in that same place.

Well, at least, I thought I broke because I couldn't speak. I can only describe it as being like I was in a dream; in another place, a different dimension. I couldn't tell anyone what I was hearing or seeing. This was way more than the man who I used to see in the hallway. I was seeing the future right in front of my face. I was hearing things and I knew exactly what to do, but I was scared to do the wrong thing. I didn't know how to express to anyone what was happening to me, so I thought that I was crazy. It was over. I was just like my mother. I thought that I would soon be muttering to myself since I couldn't talk and that my daughter would be ashamed forever.

No one could figure out what was wrong with me because when I finally did begin to speak, everything made sense. I could never admit what I saw or how I felt because I was sure that I would never be able to leave the facility if I did. I thought that I would be a patient there forever. During my time at the facility, I would lead group sessions and other patients would have private sessions with me before they went to see the psychiatrist. It was like I was a secret agent there on a mission. I knew about people's lives and I couldn't understand how or why. I was able to tell them things that helped them to work out their issues and have hope for the future. One day while in a group session, after I finally spoke up, the social worker was lost for words and could not respond to the question I posed. Then, finally, one of the other patients chimed in. "She is a social worker! She is great! She helps me!" the patient said. I was identified. The social worker ended the group session early and asked to meet with me privately in my room.

When I sat down with the social worker, it was as though she was intimidated. She admitted to me that for the first time in her career, she did not know how to help me. She believed that nothing was wrong with me, and I was discharged the next day.

Unfortunately, although I was able to know and understand things about other patients at the facility, I was unable to know and understand things about myself. I just knew that I had a way of reaching people and that I always wanted to leave them with a little hope in their hearts.

I had to get closer to God. Something was drawing me near. I wanted my life to change. At that time, my grandmother was getting sicker from cancer and was preparing me to take care of my mom. It was so hard for me to do because my mom had never taken care of me. She never changed. She still would treat me horribly, just without the spoon. The verbal abuse was just as bad and I dreaded being involved in her life.

I would still visit her in the nursing home where she resided. I attended care team meetings and made sure that she had all of her essentials, including cigarettes that I hated buying. My grandmother finally began using her wisdom to show me the importance of unconditional love. We can not choose our parents, but we can choose how we treat them. The Bible clearly says, "Honor thy mother and father: that thy days may be long...," and that was important to me because I wanted to live a long life.

I continued to visit my mother and take her to my grandmother's house for weekend visits. My daughter would also spend a great amount of time with my mother. My mother would treat her the best. I always felt like because she couldn't show me proper love growing up, she would make up for it by showing that love to my daughter. They were really close and my mom was extremely protective of my daughter. My daughter had a great relationship with both my mother and my grandmother. That made me happy. I was happy that my mother was at least able to try to be a good grandmother to make up for what she couldn't do as a mother.

My grandmother finally lost her battle to cancer. I had to become the sole provider and caretaker for my mother. By this time, all of her siblings had also passed. Even with all the pain I endured due to the verbal and mental abuse from my mom, I continued to honor her as my mother regardless of how I felt. I knew that I wanted our relationship to change. I just had to figure out how to enact that change properly.

I began a journey of healing. I wanted to get closer to God so that He could help me do so. I needed to understand how and why I was able to see, feel, and know things that not many others could. My abilities weren't common, and as I talked to more and more people, they made me realize that I was exceptional. Those who knew me throughout my life would remind me that I had always been special, even as a child.

I began to study the Bible and build a relationship with God. I struggled to attend church and I realized that religion was simply not my thing, so I joined anything I could from the comfort of my own home. I joined groups, learned how to pray and fast, and found a job that helped me to find a mission. That mission was to utilize my skills and knowledge to promote positive change.

I wanted to be free; I wanted the chains to be broken off of me. I needed to be healed from the anguish and pain I endured throughout my life.
Finally, I was able to hear what God wanted for me. I understood that I was special because I had been chosen as a vessel for God to talk to and through. He shared His thoughts about so many things with me and I was now certain that my trip to the hospital did not take place because I was "crazy." Instead, I was sent there because God wanted to show me that my mom wasn't crazy, either; she just couldn't settle the chaos and trauma she experienced and gather the strength to hear Him the way she needed to. It all made sense once I realized this, because during her schizophrenic episodes, I chose to listen to only one of her personalities. This personality was the one who I often reminded her to call me back with. She was uncommon, and when she talked, you had to listen. It always made sense; I just had to listen.

I began to listen to those things that God needed me to share with my mom. I finally forgave her, and understanding her became an easier task. I would listen more, utilizing my skills and knowledge to help her be her best. I wanted to see my mom become free from everything she had experienced. It was a lot for her. Fifty-eight years of holding onto things that she couldn't let go of had broken her down.

Still on medication at the age of fifty-eight, my mother's kidneys were destroyed. Dialysis couldn't help after several years of being on it. Her kidneys began to fail and pneumonia filled her lungs. Once I walked into her hospital room, I knew that it was the end. I was finally able to tell her to let go and not to worry what I or anyone else thought about her. She looked at me.

"April, am I about to die?" she asked me. She began to panic and wanted to explain everything. She already needed an oxygen tank and could barely talk or breathe. I stopped her immediately. I reminded her that I had already forgiven her and that it was now time for her to forgive herself.

"I forgive myself! I forgive myself! I forgive myself!" she yelled out three times through the oxygen mask.

She was finally free. I witnessed her set her spirit free. Right on her hospital bed, she was brought back to life. The nurse then walked into the room. "Please take off this mask! I don't need it; I can breathe just fine," my mother politely requested.

She was right. She was calm and her breathing was normal. I looked at my mother as she physically transformed into a beautiful angel. She was free of all of the anxiety, depression, sickness, and mental issues she suffered throughout her entire life. She had several visitors that day because the doctors had expressed to me that everything was failing and we should prepare for her passing. I wasn't afraid; her freedom gave me peace. When people walked into the room, they would say, "Wow! She is peaceful." I had never experienced witnessing someone on their deathbed with so much peace. It was especially surprising to see my mom this way, as she always seemed chaotic, anxious, and stressed. It was the oddest thing.

A few years back, my mom gave me a chain. It was one of the only things she gave me that she didn't eventually take back. I cherished that chain. She promised me that she didn't steal it, and for years, I wore it almost every day. Unbelievably, the week after she passed away, the chain broke. God spoke to me at that moment and told me that this experience was metaphorical—the chains were now broken! I cried like a baby. Finally, I was free.

This didn't mean that the chains that had once locked me down didn't leave unhealed wounds. I was still in the healing process. The scars were deep. This period led up to the COVID-19 outbreak of 2020. It was a time of make-or-break, a time of recovery, and a time to receive the essentials that I needed for my personal path. I knew that I needed to make the best of it. On the day when I decided to write this chapter of my life, I wasn't in the best of situations, but I was in a place of peace. I started to forgive everyone, including myself. I got a mentor and a therapist. I got a spiritual momma, and God is faithful. 1 Corinthians 10:13.

I escaped. I'm free. The best is yet to come.

"One small crack does not mean that you are broken, it means that you were put to the test and you didn't fall apart."
— Linda Poindexter

Chapter 9
Conswella Smith

Faith Exposed

I could not have imagined the tests of faith that I was about to experience. This should have been a time when I was enjoying life to the fullest without a care in the world, evading defeat every day with spiritual affirmations! I asked myself, Why am I still at war with myself? How did I get here? When did this happen? It was too much! There I was, in my forties, with not a single goal in my eyes even beyond sight. I was married with two children and still did not have a clue what it took to be successful. I am a failure, procrastinator, can't get right, won't do right, inconsistent… hell, I'm a mess! I told myself. Getting married in 2013 to my son's father was surely the right
thing to do.

Our trials before marriage and our growing relationship made us stronger and a super team beyond force. He became more of a man, and I became more of a woman. We both had good jobs and our kids were doing amazing in school, thanks to the awesome county education system. Together, we worked hard toward our goal to buy our first home because we were so tired of these damn rental apartments, rental homes, and rental townhouses. We were at our wit's end with anything that had the word "rent" attached to it, okay? My husband and I said that this was going to be the last time moving and that the final move would be into our new home.

I worked overtime, almost sixty hours a week, saving for a down payment. Tuition reimbursement was also set aside. This is how much we were determined to make this thang happen. I was at church every day thanking the Lord for allowing me to stay healthy for my family. Stress and fatigue had set in so heavily during the process that I thought that things might not work out for me. The devil was punching me in the face, telling me things like, "You are not going to be able to come up with the money; you are not good enough for a new house; y'all can't afford that house note; the kids are not going to like it here; you just got out of bankruptcy, they are not going to approve you; your credit score will not be high enough." I could keep going, but shoot, I am sure you get it by now.

Heard a Voice

We had almost given up at one point. All of the houses we had looked at were either snatched up because other buyers had provided better offers than we could or due to structural issues that forced us not to proceed. Then, there was this new community that I had always admired; I loved how beautiful the homes looked. I would always say, " That is where I'm going to live one day." As I was running errands, something told me to drive into the subdivision and stop by the property office. A nice, well-dressed lady greeted me as soon as I walked in and then asked if I was interested in becoming a resident of their community.

"Yes, ma'am," I said as she handed me a pamphlet that contained beautiful pictures and floor plans. Those prices were pretty, too! Pretty as in, "Aw, hell, way out of our price range." However, I still was confident—the agent and I had agreed to set an appointment with her broker. I rushed home. "Babe! I went into that new subdivision that I always spoke of. It is niiiccceee!" I told my husband.

"That nice, huh?" he asked.

"Yes," I said. This man has the most nonchalant facial expressions when he is wondering anxiously what I'm about to say next; he pretends that he is on it. If I could give him a rap name, it would be "Sir Nonchalant."

After a good, long conversation, he also agreed to speak with the broker. A few days later, I spoke with the broker and provided him with the information that he had requested in order to see if we could be prequalified. The next day, he followed up with me to give me the results. The broker stated that there were some things we still needed to do in order to qualify. He then pointed out things that were not right with our credit, among other things. I acknowledged that I understood and he asked me to give him a call in a month or so if anything changed. I was so confused and disappointed. I was already exhausted because it had been almost two years and we had yet to buy a house. I continued to stay hopeful, although still discouraged. The one thing that continuously kept me going was a constant affirmation from a pastor: "Know the voice of God, to understand my assignment, and to walk in my calling."

Little did I know that my desires were manifesting right before me at that very moment. Approximately one month later, I was sitting in my home office composing an email to a work client when I heard a voice telling me to call the broker. I kept working diligently as if I had heard nothing, then I was stopped almost abruptly as the voice came again: "Call him!" I was sitting there like, What in the world is happening? I set my status to "away—bathroom" on my system, grabbed my cell phone, and contacted the broker. I reintroduced myself, reminded him that we had spoken approximately one month ago, and told him that I just wanted to follow up on our last conversation. The broker acknowledged that he somewhat remembered our interaction, asked for my name and my husband's name, then placed me on hold. Sir, I snuck away from the PC to call you. My supervisors are already watching me. I can't return to work late, I thought to myself. He finally returned to the phone.

"Yes, Mrs. Smith, I've looked at your and your husband's file and cannot remember why I did not initially grant you preapproval in the first place," he told me. "Which model style are you interested in? You are preapproved, no matter the price, and I'm emailing your approval letter over to the agent!"

See, when you know the voice of God, things will start to announce themselves clearly in your life!

I must have run up and down my hallway almost eighteen times shouting, then I did a spin-around with my hands about twelve times, almost making myself pass out because I had not yet eaten breakfast! My husband and I felt like we were in a dream! We went through the process of choosing a lot, picking our floor plan, and designing a brand-new home that was going to be built from the bottom up. This was truly a blessing. We could not wait until our new home was completed. It took approximately three months. I would stop by the house as it was being built and write scriptures on the foundations and wood. Yes, I was building our house on the Word. On the day of closing, we were in a zone, still in disbelief. It was official! The home that I had dreamed of was about to be ours! My husband and I arrived in the parking lot. I prayed for us before walking in. The downtown attorney's office was very crowded that day. It appears that the 30th of each month is a popular day for closings. The owner of the law firm himself walked us through the signing process. Boy, it felt like we were signing our life away.

We signed about one thousand pages and initialed four hundred times. Okay, I am exaggerating a little, but shoot, it sure felt like it! It was, indeed, still a wonderful feeling. He handed us the keys as we looked at each other in awe.

It was an absolutely beautiful moment when we stepped into our new, fresh house. The carpet was super fluffy; our feet sunk into it like soft grass. The walls were freshly painted and there were neutral granite countertops, stainless steel appliances, and deep mahogany wood cabinets in the kitchen. Archways were throughout the first floor. The floor plan was so open and peaceful. We decided to surprise our kids after we picked them up from school. They were full of joy as we pulled into our two-car garage. Their bedroom sets had already arrived. We had not fully moved in, but they insisted on never going back to the old house. I chuckled my butt off. It's a wonderful feeling to see your children happy and content. We had finally made it.

Faith Leap

After almost two months of residing in our new home, my spirit began to feel heavy. I was extremely stressed due to my job as a technical support analyst. The company had been bought out and the owners, along with management, had changed drastically. I was tired and could not do it anymore. I was micromanaged to the fifth degree and the organization's morale and business had become completely intolerable. This can not be right, I told myself. Being unhappy every single day, along with experiencing fatigue and pressure, was not the business of this queen. I was determined that I had to make a change in my life and finally work on my passion, something that I loved doing and could do every day. I wanted to be my own boss and follow my dreams.

I put in my two weeks' notice without telling my husband first. I then expressed to him that I was simply unhappy and that I could not work for Corporate anymore. I told him that I was going to finally launch what I had been doing on and off for many years. This was the rebirth of A Queen's Essentials: Organic Soaps and Body Products. He agreed that if this was what I wanted, then he was behind it. I then expressed these desires with my church family and we all gathered to pray as I began my journey.

Spiritual Bottom

I was now so-called Miss Independent and I was fully excited to get started with my business. I had gathered information and now had the ultimate mindset of determination and what I thought would be the perfect plan to succeed. I had this in the bag! I am well-educated about skincare and have created and made many beauty products for sensitive skin, eczema, acne, and dry skin. You see, this hits home because I have a family history of these conditions and was determined to care for my family's skin the natural way. Why not share and introduce this to other families and communities?

Although I was a Master Cosmetologist by trade, I also had some interest in real estate. My initial plan was to also obtain my real estate license so that I would have something to fall back on. Well, that did not work.

I failed the proctor exam twice before I could even get to the real test. That sucked and I was super frustrated. There went plan B in terms of finances. We began to go downhill extremely fast. You see, we went from an income of almost $175,000 a year to $35,000. I started to see discouragement in my marriage. Going to public pantries to get food, donating plasma, and driving for Uber were just a few of the hustles that I had picked up just to try and make ends meet. I constantly asked myself, What have I done? I felt like a complete idiot! I went from saying to my children, "Yes, you have done a great job! I will buy this for you," to telling them, "No, not now, sweetie. Maybe next month." Jesus, help!!!!! I was still determined, going into salons and barbershops to ask friends for their support. I was attempting to conduct research on how to run my business with hardly any budget or clue! Oh, I was discouraged big-time at this point. I started to speak to God every day, thanking Him for still allowing my family to have a place to live and food to eat. I asked God to give me the strategies to succeed. We were behind on our mortgage and we started to receive foreclosure notices. Constant disconnection notices from our utility companies arrived in the mail while we barely kept ourselves afloat, wondering if we would, yet again, not have water for a few days. I was going to food pantries because we kept running out of food after trying to keep the lights, air conditioning, and water on.

I then began going to bioplasma centers to donate plasma so that I could keep gas in my car as I was taking the kids to and from school. One of our vehicles got repossessed. My marriage had become even more challenging. I was now feeling like a single mom instead of a wife. Doubt started to set in. Our faith was shaken. We started to argue, which led to us questioning our union.

Divine Connections

Even in the midst of my troubles, I kept going to church every Sunday and tithing. I started to connect deeply with fellow members of a support group for spiritual women and I opened to them about my struggles. Over time, I went even deeper, explaining that I never had a father figure to rely on and that I rarely felt supported in anything throughout my life, so I always invited failure and insecurities into my life. By being vulnerable with these women, I realized that I could not do this by myself, that I had to suck up my pride and seek help. Okay, I hear you, Lord. Then, it happened! My blessings started to come with divine connections! I was introduced to like-minded sisters who were involved in the cosmetology industry, as well as entrepreneurs, community leaders, and counselors. My church had been so supportive. One of my biggest concerns throughout my life was being a burden to others. I was the one who was always helping and supporting others, providing and giving from the heart. Was it now my turn? Doors and avenues opened like I had never experienced before. Angels were handling my finances, yet I did not know who they were. I was being blessed with food for my family. Two weeks before my foreclosure date was finalized, I was blessed within receiving the exact amount of money needed to save our home. I even had opportunities to vend at awesome events where I was able to introduce and sell my products.

In 2017, I became a minister at my church and decided to carry out my desire to give back to others through my entrepreneurship. I wanted to continue giving back to the community by feeding the hungry and homeless. Through the storm, God wanted me to experience how it felt to be without food. Due to my circumstances, God made me manage the small amounts of money that I had throughout my time of struggle, thus teaching me how to spend wisely and save. God gave me the strategies and tools I needed to maintain and grow my business. God gave me the words to communicate to my husband. And, finally, God gave me the strength and shield as a minister to be strong and set an example for others by sharing my testimony. I can do all things through Christ who strengthens me. No weapons formed against me shall prosper. Be not conformed to the things of this world. I am the head and not the tail. Won't He do it? Yes, He will!

"Give it to God daily... live in divine total purpose."
— C Nicole Henderson

Chapter 10
Wanda Pearson

My Struggle to Triumph with God's Grace

My Calm Before The Storm

During the 1950s, teenage pregnancy and sex education were considered taboos. It was exceedingly rare for mothers to communicate with their daughters about their menstrual cycles. My mother, Martha, got pregnant during her senior year of high school. My father, Walter, convinced her that his parents' house in Chicago, Illinois would be a safe place to have sex since no one would be home. Imagine having sex for the first time and getting pregnant. That was my mother's story, and on November 15, 1957, I was named Wanda Monette Schaefer. I would like to believe it was love at first sight for both of us.

Imagine keeping the pregnancy a secret from everyone, even the father of the child, for six months. Imagine fighting to use your voice. Teenage pregnancy can change the course of a young woman's life. It puts her in a place where she is responsible not only for herself, but also for another human being. Although my mother managed to graduate from high school during her pregnancy, raising me on her own was not the route she wanted to take. Although my mother married another man when I was one year old, I was taken in by my father and grandmother at two weeks old and was raised by them until I was five years old. As for my mother, short visitation with me was always on the table and that made me incredibly happy.

"No matter how old she may be, sometimes a girl just needs her mom."
— Cardinal Mermillod

My father later married Wilma Abrams when I was three years old and created more additions to our family, Tyrone and Torrance. I also have a sister, Lynn.

As for me, I can appreciate the love and support that my dad and Wilma provided me with over the years.

"No other love in the world is like the love a father has for his little girl."
— Unknown

When my mother married my stepfather, Clarence, they had a total of seven children. My sisters are Frankie, who was deceased at the age of twenty-five, and Carrie Ann, who is still living. My brothers are Clarence Jr. (alive) and two sets of twins: Kevin (alive) and Calvin (deceased at five years old), and Brendan (alive) and Brian (deceased at forty-nine years old).

Red Sneakers

I went to live with my mother and stepfather at the age of five to start kindergarten. We lived in a small apartment above a bar that was owned by my stepfather's father. I was so excited to start kindergarten, mostly because of my red Ked sneakers.

You know, the ones with the white strings and the white toe. Nothing was more important to me than those sneakers.

My mood quickly went from sneaker happy to devastated. A fire started in the bar below our tiny apartment and quickly spread. The red-hot flames were so high that we could not get out. It was a very scary time for me; I thought I was going to die that day. Firefighters came and rescued us! But wait!!! I had to go back and get my red Ked sneakers with the white strings and the white toe because there was nothing more important than my red Ked sneakers.

My mother stopped me in my tracks.

"Come on, Wanda, we've got to go," she said. I saw my sneakers catch on fire, which was another reason for my devastation. My mother reminded me to be thankful that we made it out alive.

"Such a person is double-minded and unstable in all they do."
— James 1:18 NIV

My kindergarten year was a terrible and trying time. Just imagine being five years old and stressed. The stress was a result of the treatment I received from my alcoholic and jealous stepfather, who was verbally, mentally, and physically abusive. There was not a time when my stepfather hesitated to activate his bad behavior toward me and my mother. We experienced the long-lasting pain of belt and extension cord whippings on our frail bodies. I remember my mother being so afraid of my stepfather that she would freeze while he abused her. His bitter insults and physical abuse felt like knives stabbing into her. The mistreatment seemed endless. When my stepfather would come home, I would try to hide, hoping he would not find me in our two-bedroom apartment and take his anger out on me. The social worker would come to our apartment to check on us. I would look at her and tell her that I wanted to be a social worker, too. That was my dream at ten years old.

My guardian angel was my cousin Pam, who was one year older than me. She would come and stay with us sometimes. Whenever she saw that I was being abused, she would call my dad's parents and have them come pick me up. She was the angel who always looked after me. I was so naive and I did not know how to say things due to fear and low self-esteem. My confidence had been taken from me. I still think of my stepfather's words: "You are nothing and you will be nothing." I thought that I was nothing because of his constant abuse. I continually asked myself, Why does he hate me so much? I believe that my mom protected me as much as she could until he would turn around to beat her so badly that her face was swollen. I could not understand why any man would hit his wife and children to make himself feel bigger, and then I realized that he could do this because no one could stop him! I would ask my mom, "Was I a mistake?" She always reassured me that I was not a mistake, but a blessing in her life. As N. K. Jemison stated, there is no greater warrior than a mother protecting her child.

Yes! That was the beginning of my struggle with life from five years old to eleven years old. Can you imagine? This is just the first part of my life, the beginning of a story waiting to unfold! I promised myself that when I got out of there, I would never again let a man hit me. The abuse caused me to never want to get married from a very young age. The abuse in my family was very depressing. I blocked out the bad things in my life during that time in an attempt to believe that there must be a better way to live.

God's Plan

"'For I know the plans I have for you,' declares the Lord, 'plans to prosper you and not to harm you, plans to give you hope and a future.'"
— Jeremiah 29:11

When I was twelve years old, my mom did something that hurt her very deeply. She released me from the abuse of my stepfather and consented to me living with my father and second mom, Wilma. We moved from Chicago, Illinois to Cleveland, Ohio. I started the eighth grade and went to a predominantly white middle school in Shaker Heights, Ohio.

I missed my mom and grandparents in Chicago and asked to move back. My dad did not want to lose me again; he did not want me to go back to what I had left. Therefore, one year later, we moved back to Illinois and I started high school at Adlai E. Stevenson High School in Buffalo Grove, Illinois.

During my three years of high school, I had to learn what diversity was all about. It was exceedingly difficult at first since I had only been exposed to my own culture during my early years, but getting to know other cultures was a different experience. I was one of four Blacks in my high school. It was a challenging and different experience for me because I had to learn how to get along with anyone, no matter what color they were. I graduated from high school at sixteen years old and went to Southern Illinois University in Carbondale, Illinois. Before I left for college, my mom's sister said to me: "Wanda, you will get pregnant while you are in college just like your mother and you will not complete college." I was so devastated that she had said that to me and I was saddened by the jealousy she felt toward me and my mom. My aunt's harsh words kept me going when I started college; I always remembered them. I felt encouraged not to let her negative words stop me from doing what God destined me to do: become a social worker and be the first one in my family to go to college. I was determined to prove her wrong and break that generational curse, the shadow looming over our family. I was determined to accomplish God's plans for me and I would not let anyone stop me from succeeding.

My Peace and Blessings are Coming

"If it is possible, as far as it depends on you, live at peace with everyone."
— Romans 12:18

My dad and second mom, Wilma, moved from Illinois to Cincinnati, Ohio during my second year of college. Later, they moved to New Jersey when I was in my third year of college in 1977.

My strength came from Wilma, who helped me to become the person who I am today, along with my mom and dad. All three of them poured into me and I am so grateful for that. Also, God always protected me by putting His angels and my family over me whenever I encountered danger. I had to learn how to get my self-esteem and confidence back, which is why I am so passionate about helping people today.

I graduated from Kean University with a Sociology/Social Work degree in 1978. My first job after college was at Mercedes-Benz.

In 1979, I was dating Dennis Pearson and I started working at Job Corps, where I counseled young and troubled women.

Dennis and I were married on August 29, 1981, and I started working for IBM Corporation on October 2, 1981.

God knew what He had brought me here to do and He knew His plans for what I was destined to do throughout my life because of the struggles I survived. I remembered my childhood dream of wanting to be a social worker and to help people. Well, look at God.

Now, this is not to say that everything got easier for me. I always had struggles, from college to married life, but I kept pushing through with God standing right beside me to pull me up onto my feet when I cried out to Him.

"Help me, Lord, to understand why my husband took our rent money to gamble it at the racetrack casino and play cards," I would pray. This caused mismanagement of money and led to challenges in our marriage. But my God is a good God because my husband changed his ways and bought our first townhouse with the savings he worked hard to earn.

I was twenty-five years old when our daughter, Danielle, was born on December 8, 1983.

I was thirty-three years old when our second daughter, Tori, was born on July 23, 1990.

The days on which our daughters came into the world were the happiest days of our lives.

"There is a time for everything, and a season for every activity under the heavens. A time to be born and a time to die, a time to plant and a time to uproot." — Ecclesiastes 3:1-2 NIV

On October 21, 2006, IBM relocated us to Atlanta, Georgia. The day after we moved, my mother, Martha, died. That was the hardest day of my life. Along with that, I had to still pay two mortgages: one in New Jersey and one in Georgia. Dennis was not working.

Lord, how can I do this? "This too shall pass."

Rainbow Joy of Blessings After the Storms

"I can do all this through Him who gives me strength."
— Philippians 4:13 NIV

Are you stuck in the way you grew up? If we are not careful, we can become prisoners of our past experiences, both good and bad. Are you a prisoner of your past? Did you decide to break the chains, or are you still wearing them? Do you want to do something different and not follow the norm, or do you want to stay stuck with the hand you were dealt?

I knew what I wanted to do over the course of my life. It was God's destiny for me to accomplish the plans He already had for me at a young age. Although I grew up in Chicago with an abusive stepfather, I knew that I did not want to have that same type of life as an adult.

Now, it took work to get my self-esteem and confidence back up, but with constant confirmation and affirmations, my second mom and God helped me to overcome everything that I had been subjected to.

My heart ached when my second mom died on March 26, 2011. My dad followed her to Heaven on March 9, 2018. I had now lost my parents, but I knew that my angels were always looking over me.

I was blessed to have my third mom, Ila Abrams, in my life.

Forgiveness in My Heart

"Be kind and compassionate to one another, forgiving each other, just as in Christ God forgave you." — Ephesians 4:32 NIV

Forgiveness is not a feeling—it is a choice. It took me decades to realize that I had not forgiven my stepdad. God put him in front of my mind when I was in a Bible class about total forgiveness.

Oh, Lord, I had no idea that those experiences were still bottled up in my mind, I thought. My husband was another person who I had to forgive. He was not working and I was faced with paying two mortgages. When I stopped worrying, I decided to let go and let God. My burdens were lifted and God stepped right into our lives. My husband was offered a job at FedEx and has been working there for twelve years. He started reading the Bible daily and our marriage became stronger. My husband and I have been married for thirty-nine years. Together, we have six grandchildren.

On December 31, 2017, I retired from IBM after thirty-six years. I have been working in our business, LegalShield, for twenty-two years after retirement. My mission in LegalShield is to educate and consult families and businesses about the value of acquiring affordable legal protection. Everyone deserves equality and justice.

So, I know that with the help of God, all things are possible. I am truly blessed and I have the audacity to shine.

"Because you have so little faith. Truly I tell you, if you have faith as small as a mustard seed, you can say to this mountain, 'Move from here to there,' and it will move. Nothing will be impossible for you."
— Matthew 17:20 NIV

No man on this earth gets to escape trials and tribulations. The trials and tribulations of my life helped me to never forget where I came from, which my father taught me. They also molded me to help others. Healing and getting my self-esteem and confidence back are possible for me, I realized. Know that there is a way out of the tunnel if you keep your mind strong and have God in your life.

"And God said, 'Let there be light,' and there was light."
— Genesis 1:3 NIV

In contributing to this book, I wanted to share the struggles that I have experienced throughout my life, but I had to ask God for strength and peace during the writing process. With God, all things are possible.

Author Biographies

C Nicole Henderson

C Nicole Henderson is an author, speaker, coach, and sought-after industry expert. She is the CEO of CNH & Associates. They offer the Clear Track 501c3 System for startup tax exempt nonprofit organizations. They also specialize in helping organizations to attain joint ventures of goodwill and social responsibility of businesses adding a nonprofit. The firm has clients in 46 states, as well as international projects. C Nicole has helped over 450 organizations. Also, her firm's niche is in helping nonprofits build earned income platforms for unrestricted funding. She successfully created social enterprise plans that yielded budgets ranging from $5,000 to six figures to millions of dollars.

She is a best-selling author of two books, Her Chronicles Volume 2 and Insider Tips for Optimal Growth in Your Business or Nonprofit.

C Nicole is a powerful and revelational teacher and speaker. She has traveled and conducted leadership sessions in varying aspects of ministry and business.

As the Dream Revelator, she has keen insight into walking in the simplicity of the Word of God and into the realms and dimensions of visions and dreams. She is a Master Scribe who walks in all three levels of The Scribal Anointing (administrative, instructional, and creative). C Nicole is an ordained prophet and licensed minister.

C Nicole is the founder of the Envision Institute, an online platform for prophetic training and leadership development. She holds two master's degrees.

IG: cnicolehenderson
Facebook: cvisionsanddreams
Twitter: DreamRevelator
Website: www.audacitytoshine.com
Linktree: Linktree.com/cnicolehenderson

Dr. Marlene Carson

Dr. Marlene Carson is a SurThriver of Domestic Minor Sex Trafficking, Member of the U.S. Advisory Council on Trafficking, Author, Coach, and Founder of Rahab's Hideaway, Rahab's Hope of Ohio, and The Switch Anti-Trafficking Network. While many have a text book knowledge of the perils faced by victims of sex trafficking, Dr. Carson knows from her own personal experience. At age fifteen, she became one of the tens of thousands of girls exploited daily. Through faith in Jesus Christ and sound biblical teaching, Dr. Carson's misery became a ministry. Her zeal has erected a vision that is unique in its application and effective in its efforts to break the cycle of exploitation, addiction, and poverty.

Stacy Bryant, also known as Coach Stacy and The Manifest Chic, is the founder of The Stiletto Bosses Network™, I Manifest Academy, and the Free Hope Foundation for Domestic Violence. She is the host of "Candid Conversation with Coach Stacy" on 108 Praise Radio. Coach Stacy is also the CEO of ICU Coaching Academy. She is a retired veteran of the United States Army and she devotes her life to empowering others. Her goal is to assist and empower people all over the world by helping them to instill and express confidence in themselves. Her focus is to empower people by helping them with their finances, relationships, entrepreneurship endeavors, health journeys, walks in faith, and lives.

Stacy is a certified Master Life Coach Trainer, best-selling author, speaker, and radio personality. Her passion for inspiring and encouraging others has made her a sought-after inspirational speaker and coach. She is the author of Building Self-Confidence and the Her Story series. Coach Stacy is also the coauthor of The Will to Win with Brian Tracy. She is also featured in four other anthologies with powerful women from all over the world. Stacy has a bachelor's degree in Business Administration and is currently pursuing her MBA.

Stacy has walked the road of an overcomer her entire life and is passionate about personal development. She is dedicated to helping others rise above their circumstances. Her mission in life is to encourage and empower others to explore and find who they are inside and out. From there, she believes they will be able to create the lives they have always dreamed of.

Sai Lena Tiona Willis

Sai Lena Tiona Willis was born to her parents, Karl Coleman and Patricia Willis, on November 10, 1986 in Pittsburg, California. Sai Lena is the middle child of six siblings between both parents. Sai Lena graduated high school and college with multiple degrees and now is a successful entrepreneur.

Sai Lena is the proud mother of Dominic Cameron. Growing up in the Bay Area, Sai Lena learned how to navigate through many dangerous situations that could have changed her story completely. Sai Lena was blessed with the opportunity to establish and form AmerCare PHS and the Princess Tiona Foundation, where she currently serves as the CEO and founder of both organizations. Sai Lena is known among all her peers as a trailblazer and pioneer as she continues to display her leadership capabilities. Through financial literacy, community outreach, or homecare, Sai Lena gives back.

Jacqueline "Lulu" Brown is a dynamic retired C-Suite Information Technology and Engineering "Thought Leader."

In 2010, Lulu's true calling and genius was burning like "fire shot up in her bones" with a revolutionary, radical and unique message for the masses of women.

Now, as an Elevation Leader, Women's Empowerment Consultant, ICF-certified Coach, and licensed Minister, she has coached and mentored women and young girls internationally. Client outcomes are alignment with spirit, authenticity, and unleashing one's divine feminine power.

Lulu values innovation, diversity, service, individuality, and equality. She believes that every woman deserves a bright shining life that sings to their soul.

Lulu hosts a weekly segment, "Be Real Be Raw Be You with Lulu: The Lulu Experience," on iWorship96 FM, an international radio station. She also hosts The Lulu Experience, a TV show which is available on the Xperience On Demand platform. Naturally philanthropic, Lulu serves on the board of The Way Out Ministries Inc., a 501c3 corporation, as their chairperson and Chief Program Officer.

Chanel Nicole Ryan
Author | Creative | Advocate | Coach

Chanel Nicole Ryan, an Atlanta-based photographer and creative writer, uses her lens and pen to tell the stories of humanity. She is the author of Things Said: A Collection of Healing Words. Shedding light on the dark place of domestic violence, Chanel is the creator of the The Purple Warrior Project, a community of survivors and advocates.

Chanel holds a Doctor of Pharmacy degree from Florida A&M University. She is a trauma recovery coach, specializing in grief, loss, and betrayal.

For over fifteen years, Toyin Fadina has dedicated her life to helping single parents and their children thrive. She is the founder of S.M.A.R.T. (Single Mothers of America Resource Team), Inc., which facilitates the needs of single parents.

Toyin serves as a professional educator and community resource, serving hundreds of single-parent families throughout metropolitan Atlanta and other areas across the globe.

She developed S.M.A.R.T. on the foundational life lessons she learned from successfully raising her daughter as a teenage mother. Through S.M.A.R.T., she uses the strategies and skills she acquired to overcome the struggles of single parenting as a testament that any single parent can rise to their full potential by taking the smart steps she has created.

www.toyinfadina.com
www.smartparentresources.org

April Sanders

April Sanders was born and raised in Asbury Park, New Jersey, and with the guidance of her strong-willed grandmother, April not only graduated high school as a teen mom, but also went on to graduate from a University with a degree in Social Work. Since an early age, April always dreamed of acting and wanted to help individuals be their best selves by utilizing her positive interpersonal skills. She believes she has a gift that can change lives and help promote positive change.

April is committed and determined to promote positive social change by doing "Heart-work" and helping to transform individual mindsets daily. She now holds a master's degree in Public Administration and is the founder of an organization called BEST (Bringing Every Strength Together). Her philosophy is, "When you know better, you do better." She is driven by the idea that in order to inspire change, we must work to change ourselves.
Romans 5:3-4

Facebook: April Sanders
Instagram: ap_real_

Conswella Smith is a master cosmetologist and skin consultant, mother, wife, and minister in Snellville, Georgia, where she is the founder and CEO of A Queen's Essentials: Organic Soaps and Natural Body Products as of 2015. She studied at the Dekalb County School of Cosmetology, where she became a licensed cosmetologist in 1999. She then went on to become a skin consultant and formulated her own natural skincare inspired by her own family's trials with recurring skin conditions. She then also became a licensed minister at New Life Church of Lithonia in 2017. Her accreditations for A Queen's Essentials include Best of Gwinnett 2018, Among the Best 2018, and Ones to Watch 2019. She was also featured in the Special Speakers Edition of Leadership TKO Magazine in March of 2019. She continues to stay involved with the community in her commitment to a homeless shelter called Hagar's House in her native location, Decatur, Georgia.

Social Media
facebook.com/aqueensessentials
instagram.com/a_queens_essentials
twitter.com/a_essentials

Wanda Pearson

Wanda Pearson is a trailblazer. With over thirty-six years of experience in marketing and sales with IBM, along with her extensive background in social work and women's counseling, Wanda's passion for helping others fuels her ministry and serves as a catalyst for her overall success. She is a consultant, entrepreneur, speaker, and thought leader on legal protection with her services she provides through LegalShield, Small Businesses, Women Empowerment, and violence against women. Wanda is a coauthor of a collaboration book titled Audacity to Shine.

Wanda has created her own company called W. D. Pearson Associates to help empower, consult with, and educate families and businesses on the best legal plans to fit their needs. As an advocate and motivational speaker, she continues to use her testimony and message to inspire people during seminars, workshops, and conferences throughout the greater Atlanta area and internationally.

Social Media
https://www.facebook.com/wanda.pearson.330
https://www.instagram.com/wpearson2/
https://www.linkedin.com/in/wanda-pearson-4062a33b/
https://twitter.com/wandapearson